Margaret Fishback Powers

FOOTPRINTS

50th Anniversary Treasury

*Stories of Compassion, Kindness, and Courage
Inspired by the Beloved Poem*

Collins

HarperCollins Publishers Ltd
2 Bloor Street East, 20th Floor
Toronto, Ontario, Canada
M4W 1A8

www.harpercollins.ca

Library and Archives Canada Cataloguing in Publication
information is available upon request.

ISBN 978-1-44342-234-5

Printed and bound in Canada
RRD 9 8 7 6 5 4 3 2 1

To my husband, Paul Laverne Powers, my first reader of the "Footprints" poem and a man who constantly lives his life with courage, with dignity, and with others in mind

Contents

Part Six: Friendship

Part Seven: Gratitude

Introduction

A WALK ON THE BEACH

Fifty years ago, in the autumn of 1964, my boyfriend, Paul (now my husband), and I took a walk on a beach—a walk that changed our lives. I told the story of that walk, and the prelude to it, in my book *Footprints: The True Story Behind the Poem That Inspired Millions*. For readers not familiar with that time in my life, I'll briefly retrace the walk on the beach and the events leading up to it.

I had spent the summer recuperating from an illness (caused by lightning) at our family home in Ontario. A relationship I had clung to came to an end, and at the time, I felt brokenhearted. Through my brother, I met Paul Powers, a youth minister who liked to use magic illusions to entertain and challenge young people.

Paul's work kept him busy, and we didn't see each other often, but we wrote lots of letters. I found I was telling him things about myself I'd never told anyone. We soon became close friends, even though miles apart.

A month later, in early autumn, Paul called to say he had been invited to speak at a youth retreat at a camp north of Kingston (about 150 miles east of Toronto), on the Canadian Thanksgiving weekend. He asked if I would accompany him and play the piano for the meetings. I happily accepted. So, on a Friday afternoon, I arrived at my sister's apartment in the west end of Toronto, where Paul and I had agreed to rendezvous. However, I wasn't prepared for what would happen when Paul arrived and then made a declaration: "I love you, and I know you love me. And I have something for you."

Surprise registered on my face as Paul opened a little black box and showed me a sparkling diamond ring, nestled in velvet. Paul says my expression was at first sheer delight but that it almost turned to shock. I was a rather old-fashioned young woman in many respects and was accustomed to doing things in a very traditional way. I knew my parents had come to love Paul, but were they ready to welcome him into the family? It was all so sudden!

As it turned out, the ring was much too large for my finger. Paul slipped it on, and then we stood there laughing at the way it spun around. It was size six, and I was size three. "I'll speak to your parents and get your father's consent when we get back," he said thoughtfully. "Does that make you feel better?"

Soon, we were on our way to the Echo Lake conference grounds, near Kingston.

ψ

PAUL AND I WERE TO MEET several carloads of young people in Kingston for coffee before caravanning on to Echo Lake, some twenty miles farther. We were early, so we decided to go for a walk on the beach. Born and raised in the Great Lakes area, I have always loved beaches and sand hills. Paul parked the car and we jumped out, leaving behind our shoes, and went off barefoot, squishing the warm sand between our toes as we ran along.

The late afternoon sun dancing on the water made it sparkle. It was incredibly beautiful! As we chatted, we held each other's hand and dashed in and out of the water while the waves rolled up on shore. Finally Paul looked at his watch and said it was time to turn back.

We laughed and made more light talk, retracing our steps toward the car, and then, when we picked up our discussion, it took a serious turn. The waves were washing up over our footprints, leaving only one set of prints visible. "Maybe that's what will happen to us—maybe we'll be all washed up," I said, sighing. "Maybe our dreams are going to wash away."

"No," Paul protested, "this makes me think of our future. On our wedding day, we two will become one. See our footprints just up ahead? They're still there. Where they are washed out, that means troubled waters we're going to face. Every marriage faces that. We have to work at marriage every day."

"What will happen when trouble comes that we just can't handle?" I asked. We paused and I pointed to the sand. "Look, Paul, now there's only one set of footprints!"

Paul fell silent for a moment, then he said, "Margie, when the most troublesome times come, times that neither one of us can handle, that's when the Lord will carry us both, as long as we maintain our faith and trust in Him."

It was such a beautiful thought, expressed with such utmost sincerity, that it took my breath away. The poet in me stirred. How could I let this man go? Then he playfully picked me up, and put me on his shoulder.

We were young and in love, serious and contemplative, but the retreat was to be a happy event and Paul enjoyed hearing me laugh and seeing me smile. He knew that I needed this weekend retreat as much as any of the students who would be attending. He reminded me, "I'm here. I'm holding you, and you're safe."

It all happened in the space of just a few minutes, but the impression and memory have lasted forever. I remember how Paul gently put me down—how we kept walking, arms around each other's waist. But as we walked, we continued to silently observe our two sets of footprints—and sometimes one. And it set my mind to musing. I was quite absorbed in my thinking.

We returned to the hotel, where we were to meet the others. As we sat in the coffee shop waiting for them to arrive, I took a paper napkin and began jotting down some ideas and phrases.

"What are you doing?" Paul asked, as if he didn't already know. He'd seen me reach for something to write on when the inspiration struck. Poems were always forming in my head, it seemed.

"Oh, just another poem," I said, smiling at him. "It's about our footprints in the sand."

⚛

WHEN THE YOUNG PEOPLE ARRIVED, we all piled into our cars and drove on to Echo Lake. We found our cabins and unpacked. That evening, we enjoyed music and Paul spoke at the conference meeting. Then I went to our large open cabin. The girls were having fun, but I was tired from a very long day and the drive from Toronto. Many of the other girls were tired, too, having traveled from New York State. I was glad when they settled down and one by one fell asleep. Yet sleep eluded me.

I thought about Paul and wondered if our relationship had proceeded too fast. We'd known each other only six weeks. What would my family say? My mind replayed our beach-walk conversation. And then I reached for my notepad, pen, and flashlight. The words that had been forming in my head since that afternoon began taking shape on the paper.

As if in a dream, I saw a story unfolding in my mind's eye. I saw myself walking along a beach with the Lord, our feet leaving footprints in the sand. Across the sky flashed scenes from my life, and for each scene, I noticed two sets of footprints in the sand— my own, and that of the Lord. When the last scene of my life shot before me, I looked back and saw that there was only one set of footprints. I realized that this was at the lowest and saddest times of my life. I asked the Lord where He had been when I needed Him most.

The words tumbled out, easily, effortlessly. "Lord, You told me when I decided to follow You, You would walk and talk with me all the way. But I'm aware that during the most troublesome times of my life, there is only one set of footprints. I just don't understand why, when I needed You most, You leave me."

Then I wrote his reply:

He whispered, "My precious child,
I love you and will never leave you,
never, ever, during your trials and testings.
When you saw only one set of footprints,
it was then that I carried you."

Suddenly, I was aware that I was writing free verse, which was not at all usual for me. I was accustomed to writing in rhyming verse or couplets.

I looked at my watch. It was 3 a.m. I shivered, feeling the cool early-morning air. "You'd better get some shut-eye," I told myself. Just before falling asleep, I thought, *Now I've written this and I don't even have a title.* Then I wondered, *Has this just been a dream?*

In the morning, upon awakening, I reached for the notepad, read the poem, and immediately the thought came: *You should call it "I Had a Dream."*

And that's how I wrote the poem all those years ago. It came to be known by the title "Footprints," but to us, it will always be a reminder of our beach walk. To us, it symbolizes the time when we realized that God was saying that this would be a God-blessed marriage, and that He would always be there walking with us, carrying us when we need to be carried—as, of course, He wants to do for all His children.

FOOTPRINTS IN THE SAND

One night I dreamed a dream.
I was walking along the beach with my Lord.
Across the dark sky flashed scenes from my life.
For each scene, I noticed two sets
of footprints in the sand,
one belonging to me
and one to my Lord.

Margaret Fishback Powers

When the last scene of my life shot before me
I looked back at the footprints in the sand.
There was only one set of footprints.
I realized that this was at the lowest
and saddest times of my life.
This always bothered me
and I questioned the Lord
about my dilemma.

"Lord, You told me when I decided to follow You,
You would walk and talk with me all the way.
But I'm aware that during the most troublesome
times of my life there is only one set of footprints.
I just don't understand why, when I needed You most,
You leave me."

He whispered, "My precious child,
I love you and will never leave you,
never, ever, during your trials and testings.
When you saw only one set of footprints,
it was then that I carried you."

As long as I can remember, I have written and recorded events and emphasized just what I have learned from various situations. I have catalogued the proof that God can use even our most painful experiences in life to make us stronger and more useful to Him.

When we decided to celebrate the 50th anniversary of the poem "Footprints in the Sand" with a treasury of stories, we asked contributors to submit stories inspired by the poem. That was the only requirement. We were humbled by the number of wonderful pieces that friends and strangers wrote. And though we first wondered if the submissions would be "all over the map," we were surprised—and delighted—to see that they shared several common themes: compassion; hope, trust, and faith; burdens, courage, and strength; goodness and gentleness; kindness and comfort; friendship; and gratitude. These themes are woven through the book like the threads of a rainbow tapestry.

I trust that you will enjoy meeting real people with real stories about real events that have happened in their lives. Some of these stories are about life-changing experiences, while others tell of small, everyday kindnesses that made a lasting impression. Some stories will bring a tear to the eye, others a smile to your face. You'll find, I hope, that truth is often more interesting than fiction. (That's why I'm a nonfiction writer.)

KINDNESS IS A VERY BEAUTIFUL WORD. It is derived from the Greek word *chrestotes*, which means moral goodness and integrity.

I have often thought that the kindest people are those who have no ambition to be kind and make no plans to be so. This is not to say that they don't desire to be kind. Rather, they don't try to manufacture their kindness. They don't think, *Oh, look at me and what I did.* Rather, they consider how they can reflect their Lord to a hurting world.

The person whose kindness is an appetite for praise gives up when the adulation doesn't arrive. The person whose kindness flows out of his or her relationship with God never gives up. That person just can't help being kind. Such kindness is what we see in the stories shared in this book.

The following is more a thought than a poem, but it is very meaningful for me. I wrote it as a young woman. These many years later, I feel it reflects the essence of this book.

A Heart for Him
Thoughtfulness
Hand extended in help
Answer to prayer
Not asking for returns
Kindness that remains

Known only to Him
Obedience to God
Unselfishness and unconditional Love
To look after His child

—Margaret Fishback Powers

PART ONE
Compassion

But You, O Lord, are a God full of compassion, and gracious,
Longsuffering, and abundant in mercy and truth.
     —Psalm 86:15

And Jesus, when He came out, saw a great multitude and was
moved with compassion for them, because they were like sheep
not having a shepherd. So He began to teach them many things.
     —Mark 6:34

He who has pity on the poor lends to the Lord,
And He will pay back what he has given.
     —Proverbs 19:17

Indeed we count them blessed who endure. You have heard of the
perseverance of Job and seen the end intended by the Lord—that
the Lord is very compassionate and merciful.
     —James 5:11

Remember, O Lord, Your tender mercies and Your loving
     kindnesses,
For they are from of old.
     —Psalm 25:6

Then He said, "I will make all My goodness pass before you, and I
will proclaim the name of the Lord before you. I will be gracious

to whom I will be gracious, and I will have compassion on whom I will have compassion."
—Exodus 33:19

Then Jesus answered and said, "A certain man went down from Jerusalem to Jericho, and fell among thieves, who stripped him of his clothing, wounded him, and departed, leaving him half dead . . .

"But a certain Samaritan, as he journeyed, came where he was. And when he saw him, he had compassion.

"So he went to him and bandaged his wounds, pouring on oil and wine; and he set him on his own animal, brought him to an inn, and took care of him."
—Luke 10:30, 33–34

Through the Lord's mercies we are not consumed,
Because His compassions fail not.
They are new every morning;
Great is Your faithfulness.
—Lamentations 3:22–23

DO MORE THAN CARE

Do more than belong: participate. Do more than care: help. Do more than believe: practice. Do more than be fair: be kind. Do more than forgive: forget. Do more than dream: work.

—William Arthur Ward

A good character is the best tombstone. Those who loved you and were helped by you will remember you when forget-me-nots have withered. Carve your name on hearts, not on marble.

—Charles H. Spurgeon

Compassion will cure more sins than condemnation.

—Henry Ward Beecher

By compassion we make others' misery our own, and so, by relieving them we relieve ourselves also.

—Thomas Browne, Sr.

Compassion helps to heal the hurts in and from others.

—Geoff Still

People may excite in themselves a glow of compassion, not by toasting their feet at the fire, and saying, "Lord, teach me compassion," but by going and seeking an object that requires compassion.

—Henry Ward Beecher

The purpose of life is not to be happy. It is to be useful, to be honorable, to be compassionate, to have it make some difference that you have lived and lived well.

—Ralph Waldo Emerson

We must never minimize the suffering of another. Scripture's mandate to us is, Weep with those who weep (Romans 12:15).

—Billy Graham

A Poem for Arthur

Arthur Thompson

Our lives take different twists and turns. But sometimes, two people's paths intersect unexpectedly—and perhaps that happens for a reason.

Last Sunday was a perfect autumn day in Toronto. I decided to walk through the park, enjoy the fall colors of the trees reflected in Grenadier Pond, and then do some shopping.

After crossing the park, I walked along Bloor Street, stopping for a coffee and then continuing along my way. There's a fascinating international stretch of the street that includes Mexican, Nicaraguan, Ethiopian, Portuguese (and other) restaurants and stores.

At a fruit store, a gentleman struck up a conversation when he saw me buying local everbearing raspberries. His hands were shaking and he was unsteady on his feet, using a cane that was obviously too small, but he spoke animatedly, telling me about picking wild raspberries as a young boy in Newfoundland. Then he described the taste of partridgeberries. And blueberry wine. Before long, we were sitting together on a bench, and I asked where in Newfoundland he was from. "Port au Port Peninsula," he said. I told him I had a sister-in-law from that area, and before long we were exchanging stories about our backgrounds.

His hands continued to shake uncontrollably. His speech patterns were erratic, but I was immensely enjoying our conversation immensely; it soon covered books, music, politics, and life in a large city. He paused for a moment and then told me he was a drug addict—he badly wanted to kick his addiction, though he knew it wouldn't be easy, and was hoping to get into a detoxification center.

We introduced ourselves and, coincidentally, discovered we shared a name: Arthur. He told me his age—young fifties, just a few years younger than I was.

I felt that we could have been friends. I don't know what drove him to drugs, and it wasn't my place to ask. Perhaps he had been dealt a poor hand in life. But we had similar interests; he had the kind of quirky sense of humor I enjoy, and he seemed sincere.

I told the man that I wished him well, and then explained that I would never preach to him—it wasn't my style. But I said that I didn't think it was a coincidence that we had met, or that we shared a name. Then I reached into my pocket for my wallet— not for money, but for a folded piece of paper that I kept tucked away in a hidden compartment.

On that paper, which I carried with me as a gentle reminder that in times of hardship I am not alone, was the poem "Footprints in the Sand." I handed it to Arthur as we said good-bye.

I have no idea if Arthur carried out his plan to go to a detoxification center—I can't begin to imagine his struggle, or the demons he has faced in his life. And though of course I don't know if he looked at the words on the paper that I handed him, I hope he did, and that they gave him strength.

Roses Are Red

Eva Schatz

A small act of compassion, remembered for a lifetime.

Following the Hungarian Revolution against the Soviet Union in 1956, thousands of my countrymen were arrested and many were imprisoned. About two hundred thousand Hungarians, my family among them, fled the country as refugees.

Through the help of a church, our family settled in a poor area of the Bronx. We were crowded in an apartment—my parents, my grandmother, my two brothers, and me. Our clothes were donated by the kind people in the church. Our sponsors were Protestant and we were Catholic. It didn't matter.

I spoke a little English and was sent to a public school. Being ten years old, I was placed in the fourth grade. The teacher, Miss Simon, was very kind and tried to get the children to talk to me. She spent time after school helping me with my English.

Some of the children in the class tried to be friendly, in an awkward way, but I didn't have time to stay around after my lessons. My father, who had been a teacher in Hungary, had found a job in a restaurant, and my mother, a scientist, now worked in a dry-cleaning store. My grandmother, brothers, and I were at home during the day. Grandma made the meals and looked after the apartment. The three children helped a little, but mostly we were encouraged to do our schoolwork and to read. We had no television, just an old radio.

At the end of the school year, all the kids were excited about going to camp, a concept that was quite foreign to me. Also foreign to me were some of the customs the children had. The strangest one was the "autograph book." This was a blank book, about four by six inches, with pages in different colors. My schoolmates exchanged their books with each other and wrote silly messages on the pages. These messages made no sense to me: "Yours till the kitchen sinks." "Yours till the horse flies." "Yours till Niagara Falls." Teachers and older relatives wrote more serious words—I remember something about a "wise owl" living in a tree.

The boy whose desk was next to mine asked me to write a few words in his autograph book. I didn't know what to say, so I just signed my name. Then he asked if he could write in my book. I was embarrassed and explained that I didn't have one.

Our family had trouble finding money for rent, food, and clothes—the idea of writing silly messages on blank pages seemed frivolous. Yet for a moment, I wanted to be just like my class-mates. I wanted to go to camp. I wanted to have nicer clothes. I wanted my parents to have more time to spend with us. And I wanted an autograph book.

That night when I went to bed, I felt sorry for myself. I knew I was lucky that our family had left a troubled country. And I knew they were right when they told us we would have a good future. But I felt completely alone. I would probably never again see Anna, my best friend from Budapest. As for new friends—would I ever have any?

The next day, the boy who had asked me to sign his book sat in the chair beside mine and whispered that he wanted to give me something at recess. He was usually shy, but today he had a big smile on his face. During recess, he handed me a small cardboard box. I opened it carefully. Inside was something square and cov-ered in pink vinyl with a little clasp that, when you unlocked it, opened into a book with multicolored pages. It was an autograph book—just like everyone else's. I thanked the boy awkwardly and put my little gift into my schoolbag.

That night at home, I looked at the empty book. I turned each page, thinking about my future life in this faraway place and wondering how things would work out for my family. Each blank page reminded me of how unsure I was and how uncertain our future would be. I turned the pages—blue, pink, yellow—each one empty. But then, in the middle of the autograph book, on a pale blue page, I saw some writing.

I read the words:

Roses are red, violets are blue,
Sugar is sweet, and so are you.
Welcome to your new country. You are going to like it here.
Your friend,
Sam

For the first time in two months, I smiled. Everything was going to be all right.

The Pharmacy

Alan Baker

Sometimes, we feel we know people though we have never met them. Sometimes, they touch our lives in ways we never expect. Sometimes, they surprise us with the depth of their feelings and understanding—and we realize then that they are easing our burden.

My mom suffered from Parkinson's disease. She struggled for many years but maintained her grace and sense of humor. It was my privilege to help look after her. I told friends that it was little trouble for me to look after Mom because of her generally pleasant nature. It also helped that I worked at home. During the last years, we were lucky to have some special home-care workers.

Neighbors who saw Mom and me in the elevator always enjoyed chatting with her. And, to be honest, there were some benefits for me. I was newly divorced, and I was happy to be able to do something fulfilling. I know that some people took a liking to me because of my mom. Folks in the building who barely knew me invited me to parties—I suspect I never would have been asked had it not been for my reputation as a "good son."

I tried to take Mom out as much as possible, but given her illness and her age, she was largely housebound. We took short walks when she had the energy. Doctors' appointments were a highlight—Mom enjoyed the drive and loved to chat with people, especially kids, in the waiting room.

Mom had never taken much medicine—it had always been a source of pride for her that she "never took a pill." But as the Parkinson's advanced, the dosage increased. It seemed as if I was spending a lot of time at the pharmacy, dropping off prescriptions and picking up meds.

There were two clerks at the pharmacy: Nelly and Hanna. Hanna was the friendly one. She'd often ask how I was, and she understood that I was usually in a hurry. She'd see me walking to the counter and, if she was free, would package the pills and have them ready when I got there. Sometimes she'd ask how I was, or how my mother was doing—even though she had never met her. Occasionally we chatted. I learned that she was from a small town in the Philippines and deeply missed many of her family members who were still there. Nelly was less personal. Given my frequent appearances, she knew who I was and always acted professionally. But she rarely smiled, never acted in a warm manner, never shared anything about her life or asked about mine.

Mom passed away shortly after her ninety-first birthday. On

Wednesday night, she enjoyed a bowl of strawberry ice cream—her favorite—and read the newspaper. On Thursday, she had difficulty breathing. An ambulance took her to the hospital, and she died two days later.

It was a difficult period for me. Mom was ready to go, but I wasn't quite prepared to say good-bye. We had always been close—my dad had passed away when I was a teenager, and I was then the only child still at home. Mom worked hard to make sure I had a good education and upbringing.

I donated Mom's clothes as she had wished and settled up all those things that needed to be settled. A nearly full bottle of pills remained on the medicine cabinet shelf. I was told the pharmacy would dispose of them properly.

Both Hanna and Nelly were at the counter when I arrived—this time I was returning meds, rather than picking them up. Both women understood at a glance what that meant. "I'm sorry," Hanna said quietly as I handed her the pills. But it was Nelly who reached for my hand, then quickly turned away, grabbed a tissue, and sobbed for a very long time.

The Letter Writer

~~~~~

Charles Mueller

Often we forget that a loved one feels lonely and isolated. Then a child helps break down a barrier.

I'd like to tell you about my brother Ronald. He was always a mischievous kid—and, now in his fifties, he still has a mischievous streak. He loves telling jokes, and our nephews call him "funny Uncle Ronnie." But ever since he was a child, he has had a heart of gold. Even then he did good deeds and never bragged about them. But occasionally they'd come to light.

We had two older neighbors—Irv and Eva Turner. They both spoke with thick accents. Mrs. Turner had a reputation for being crusty, and Mr. Turner was a quiet type. But Ronnie was always friendly with them, and one day Mrs. Turner asked if he could help write a couple of letters for them. Ronnie often got into trouble at school, but he was a bright kid—and the neighbors knew it. Before long, Ronnie was spending a couple of hours a week at the Turners'. He would have been about twelve years old at the time. The Turners looked ancient to us, but they were probably in their fifties or young sixties. They were from Poland, had come to Toronto after the war, and had a married son but no grandchildren.

Ronnie was happy to be the letter writer for the Turners. Mrs. T. was an excellent baker, and there were always homemade cookies and other goodies waiting at the end of the letter-writing session.

Ronnie sometimes wrote letters to the telephone or electric company—especially if the Turners were disputing a charge. Once, the Turners planned a holiday and Ronnie wrote a letter to the resort asking for the "particulars" about the place. Ronnie also wrote to the Turners' son, who lived in a nearby town. Ronnie would tell me how the Turners would complain in their letter that their son never phoned them, never wrote to them, and never visited. They thought he was a big shot, and while they were proud of him, they didn't hesitate to tell him off. Also, they didn't very much like the son's wife. If Mrs. Turner mentioned her in the letter, it was just to say she was sure she spent a lot of time—and money—shopping, and probably didn't know how to cook very well.

Mrs. Turner did all the dictation, and occasionally Mr. Turner tried to chime in with a few words. After Ronnie had written a letter, Mrs. Turner would sign it and Ronnie would put it in the envelope, address it, stick on a stamp, and then have some cookies or a piece of cake with a tall glass of milk.

Although the Turners complained that their son never visited, we knew that he showed up from time to time. And, during one of those visits, we learned something that Ronnie had never told us.

After visiting his parents that day, the Turners' son rang our bell. Our parents knew him slightly, and they invited him inside. From the way he dressed and spoke, we could tell he was successful—perhaps in his thirties and likely holding a prestigious position in his company. He drove an expensive car, and his manners were perfect. My folks invited him to join us at the kitchen table, and my mom put on a pot of coffee. I sat with them. Ronnie wasn't home—he was probably out with his friends, getting into a little trouble.

Neil, the son, said he had something he wanted to show us. From the inside pocket of his jacket, he took out a folded sheet of lined paper. He unfolded it and placed it on the table. We recognized Ronnie's handwriting—large letters, but neat. It was obviously a letter that Neil's mother had dictated to Ronnie. But it wasn't anything like the type of letter Ronnie had described to me.

Neil smiled as he leaned forward and started to read from the letter:

Dear Son,

Your father and I are sitting alone in our apartment. How are you? We know you are busy. Our neighbors' son Ronnie is writing this letter for us because his English is better than ours. He's a good boy. I bake him cookies. He loves them. You used to like them, too—the kind with the poppy seeds.

We are having cold weather, and it is hard for us to get out and do our shopping. Last night we watched *Bonanza*—we both love Little Joe! He's such a good son, and so nice looking. We weren't crazy about the guests on Carson's show—we don't seem to know who any of them are.

The phone company is giving us trouble—the bill was very high last month, and we try not to make long-distance calls. We get nervous talking too long and thinking about the bill. I don't think we spoke as long as they said we did.

We haven't heard from you in a long time. Are you all right? Please look after yourself—we love you very much. We know you are busy, but it would be nice to receive a letter. We would like to see you. We're getting older, you know. How is your pretty wife?

We're having meat loaf for dinner tonight. It's your favorite. Would your wife like the recipe?

Love,

Your mom and dad

My parents said it was a nice letter, but they were a little confused about why Neil had read it to them.

Neil refolded the letter and tucked it into his jacket pocket. He smiled broadly. "That's definitely not the way my mom talks," he said. "And I'm not referring to her difficulty with English." He laughed and continued, "I think our young letter writer has added a few touches."

"Oh, dear," Mom said. "Our Ronnie can be a little mischievous. I'll talk to him as soon as I see him. He probably didn't know what he was doing."

"I wish you wouldn't say anything," Neil replied. "I have a feeling your son knew *exactly* what he was doing. I can't tell you how glad I am that I saw my folks today—and the letter writer knew just how to get me to visit them."

Life Lessons

Hilda Weill

So many lessons are best learned through example.

Our mom did things in a quiet way. She never touted her good deeds. Indeed, she never thought of them as good deeds—compassion was a natural part of her life. When, as a child, I whined because I thought my brother didn't thank me sufficiently for something I had helped him with, she quietly explained what it meant to do something "graciously." That was one of my greatest life lessons.

After our mom passed away, I heard from several of the people she had helped during her years as a hospital volunteer.

A woman named Mary wrote a note to the hospital and asked that it be forwarded to our family.

"I believe in angels, having met your mom," she wrote. "Two years ago, I had surgery for a cancerous thyroid. They operated twice in three weeks, and both times I had the pleasure of your mom's company—she escorted me to my room. The night before my second surgery, when I was at my lowest point, I opened my eyes and there she was—with a smile and kind words. That was when I knew for sure there really are angels."

A True Florence Nightingale

Lois Simpson

Kind and compassionate care will live in the heart forever.

It was 11 a.m. on February 8, 1976. I went into premature labor with my third child. My husband was working, so I called a friend to take me to Hamilton's Henderson General Hospital and my mom to babysit my two young children. My doctors determined it was too early for me to have the baby. Because he felt that the baby's lungs had not yet had sufficient time to develop, I was given straight alcohol intravenously to stop the labor. I stayed in the hospital for the next three days.

Over a month later, on March 16, I was back at Henderson. Because I had no contractions, doctors decided to induce labor. The following morning, they told me labor had not yet begun. I begged to differ with them. I had been in labor all night long.

At about twelve fifteen in the afternoon, the hard labor began and the doctors attempted to do an epidural. But it didn't take, and the contractions became even stronger.

Had it not been for an amazing nurse, I don't know how I would have gotten through the following hours. She said to me, simply and calmly, "My dear, you are going to have this child naturally." At the time, natural childbirth was neither usual nor encouraged.

And then it began. I was in agony! I never really looked at the nurse's face, since I could concentrate only on the excruciating pain and her rock-solid arm, which she told me to bear down on as much as I needed to. Her soothing voice constantly reassured me that we would get through this ordeal together. The nurse stood beside me and said again, "Hold onto my arm, and just press as hard as you need to."

It was now time to change shifts. Other nurses came to the nurse and said, "You need to go or you will miss your bus. We'll take over." But my Florence Nightingale just responded to them, "Go away. I am staying until this woman has her baby. I am not leaving her until this child is born."

To this day, I think that nurse still has the scars on her arm from how hard I pressed my nails into it. She stayed with me in the labor room, then walked with me as they steered me into the delivery room. I believe her shift was over at 3 p.m. My third child, Darlene, was born at almost 5 p.m.

I was never able to thank my guardian angel nurse who helped me deliver Darlene because she must have had a few days off. I was in the hospital for four days and was not able to find out who she was. The kind and compassionate care I received that day will live in my heart forever. It must have been divine intervention.

They say that the childbirth experience is immediately forgotten once your healthy child emerges into the world. I disagree. This experience is still vivid in my mind—not because of the pain, but because of the compassion of an anonymous nurse.

Finding a Doctor

Jane Serlin

Concern, encouragement, belief, and "tough words"—together, they can play a part in our healing.

I would be seeing a surgeon for a minor procedure. My doctor had recommended him highly, but I'm the kind of person who likes to do "due diligence." So I went on the Internet and searched his name. About ten people had rated his skills—and his ratings were, thankfully, high. But what caught my eye was this comment from an anonymous former patient:

"Today I celebrate fifteen years of sobriety. Not a single slip. After thirty years of serious drinking, I have this remarkable doctor to thank. While I was hospitalized, Dr. R. not only (justifiably) told me off for allowing myself to reach the stage I was in, but he also put the fear of God in me. Most importantly, he believed in me and convinced my wife to do the same. It was his faith in my tenacity to straighten myself out and his genuine concern and encouragement that, in turn, gave my wife her belief in my capacity to succeed. This unquestionably got me to where I am today, a proud grandfather and the head of a flourishing business. I am forever grateful. Without Dr. R., I very much doubt I would be here today to write this long-overdue note of thanks to him."

I knew I would be in good hands.

The Caregiver

Vincent Rosner

What being "the best" really means.

Yesterday was a medical day. First thing in the morning, I had to be at the lab for some routine blood work. That would be followed by a visit to the hospital, where my friend Alex had an appointment with a cancer specialist.

I arrived at the lab at about 8 a.m. The earlier I go, the earlier I can leave—and head to the coffee shop for much-needed caffeine following my fast. When I arrived, the waiting room was about half full. I signed in, took a seat, and picked up a magazine while waiting for my turn with the technician.

Several more people arrived, including a frail older woman accompanied by her middle-aged daughter. The older woman appeared upset and confused, but the younger woman comforted her. "Have a seat, Mama," she said. "I'll be right back."

The daughter then went to the desk and handled the paperwork quickly before returning to sit with her mother. I was struck by the way she comforted her mom. Over the years, I've spent a lot of time in waiting rooms and have observed caregivers with their parents—some are patient, some less so. I understand the stress, but I find it sad to see a child talk disrespectfully to a parent.

The older woman, although now less agitated, was still confused. Her daughter spoke to her in another language—Polish, I think it was—and then softly sang to her. Within moments, the mother's face was transfixed. She was smiling sweetly as, I imagine, she returned to a time long ago. Perhaps she was a little girl on a farm, or spending time with her own mother or grandmother. But the change in her eyes, from pain and worry to contentment and peace, was magical.

I knew I could wait a few extra minutes for coffee and suggested to the daughter that her mom go ahead of me. The daughter thanked me profusely, and the mom gave me a smile worth so much more than the value of my small gesture.

The daughter accompanied her mom into the technician's cubicle. I heard her gently reassure her mother. A few minutes later, they left the lab. I assumed the daughter was a full-time caregiver to her mom. She didn't seem rushed to get to a job, or distracted by work-related thoughts. How fortunate, I thought, to be able to be in such a position.

It was soon my turn, and before I knew it, I was out of the lab and heading to the coffee shop.

My next stop was at a downtown hospital to visit Alex, one of my closest friends. Alex and I had been college chums but we had lost touch for about ten years following graduation, when his job took him to another city. Then, about five years ago, he returned to Toronto. A week later, we bumped into each other on the subway. We arranged to meet for coffee, caught up on our lives, and stayed close from then on. He'd been there for me through a couple of rough patches. Now it was my turn. He was on his own, having never married.

Alex was seeing a new doctor, a surgeon said to be the top specialist in the type of cancer he had. Told that the tumors he had were inoperable, Alex would be meeting with this doctor to discuss his treatment options over the coming months. He had asked me to be there for the consultation. "I'm not sure I'll register everything that I hear or express myself quite the way I want to," he had said to me. "And I need a friend to be there."

Alex's family doctor had explained that the specialist was "the best—absolutely cutting edge." She would be familiar with the latest treatments, some of them experimental. Alex had no illusions of a miracle cure, and he knew what he did *not* want: a heavily invasive course of medical treatment that would do nothing for the quality of his life. He would rather "bow out gracefully," as he put it. Unfortunately, his cancer had been diagnosed late and was progressing aggressively. He wanted to make his thoughts clear to the doctor, but he was also open to treatment ideas. He was worried that the doctor would be brilliant but impersonal; would not communicate well and be rushed; would be concerned more about the latest technology and "life-saving interventions" than with what the patient really wanted.

We sat in the waiting room outside the doctor's office, Alex and I. I didn't know if I should chat or just sit with him and offer quiet support. Finally I picked up a magazine. As I skimmed the pages, I heard footsteps coming into the room. "Mr. Thompson," a woman's voice said. "I'm Dr. Novak. Would you like to step into my office so we can chat?"

The voice sounded strangely familiar, but I couldn't quite place it. Then I looked up from my magazine and immediately recognized the face. It belonged to the loving daughter I had seen at the lab, just a few hours earlier.

101 Acts of Random Kindness and Compassion

Various Contributors

Three things in human life are important: the first is to be kind; the second is to be kind; and the third is to be kind.

—Henry James

The best portion of a good man's life is his little, nameless, unremembered acts of kindness and of love.

—William Wordsworth

1. Say something special to everyone you meet during the next twelve hours.
2. Offer a cold drink or a piece of fruit to a delivery person.
3. Send someone a small gift anonymously.

4. Write a poem or song for someone.
5. Compliment coworkers on their job performance or their positive attitude.
6. Prevent a possible accident. If you see a banana peel on the street, pick it up. Or let someone know if their shoelace is untied.
7. Change your seat on a plane, train, or bus so that friends or family members can sit together.
8. Give up your seat on the bus for someone—not just an older person.
9. Cut your neighbor's hedge or mow their lawn.
10. Help someone move or decorate.
11. Include other people—especially those who are shy—in talks and discussions.
12. If you're an employer, let your staff go home early one day.
13. Visit a grandparent.
14. Keep an extra pair of gloves in your pocket and offer them to a gloveless stranger on a cold day.
15. Pick up some litter.
16. Surprise a neighbor with a bouquet of flowers or a basket of vegetables from your garden.
17. Strike up a conversation with a classmate or neighbor you don't know well.
18. Be a friend to a newcomer at work.

19. Offer your professional expertise to someone who's just starting out in the workforce.
20. Thank a parent (even if your mom or dad is no longer alive).
21. Lend a hand to someone struggling with heavy bags.
22. Donate gently used toys to a shelter.
23. Eat lunch with a newcomer at work or school—and share your dessert.
24. Help shovel your neighbor's snow or clean their icy windshield.
25. Share magazines when you finish reading them.
26. Tell friends or family members how much you appreciate something they did.
27. Volunteer for an organization that needs help.
28. Give someone the benefit of the doubt.
29. Offer to walk a neighbor's dog.
30. Buy an inspirational book for a friend and write a personal inscription in it.
31. Help an elderly neighbor carry out the garbage . . . or roll in the neighbor's trash cans after garbage pickup.
32. Do you play a musical instrument? Contact a seniors' center or a hospital and offer to give a recital.
33. Forgive someone (and remember to forgive yourself).
34. Offer to fill in for a caregiver, allowing him or her some respite.

35. Send a valentine on the 14th day of the month—even if it's June and not February.
36. Tell your coworkers (or your employees, or your bosses) how much you appreciate them.
37. A little appreciation goes a long way—provide Vitamin E for "encouragement."
38. Organize a potluck at work to mark a special event (or for no special reason).
39. Leave a thank-you note for your letter carrier or newspaper delivery person.
40. Suggest a job idea to someone looking for a position.
41. Treat a friend to the movies . . . for no reason.
42. Call a lonely person.
43. Make someone happy.
44. Give your flowers to the living. If you hear a compliment about someone, pass it along.
45. Let your parents know why you love them.
46. Volunteer your time and skills.
47. Congratulate (or comfort) a teammate—depending on the outcome of the game.
48. Donate your gently used clothes or books to an organization.
49. Don't underestimate the power of a hug. Hug a friend!
50. Give someone your full attention when they speak.
51. Invite someone who lives alone to dinner.

52. Thank your brother or sister or cousin for a past kindness.
53. Attend an event that's important to a friend or relative.
54. Come to work early and make coffee for your coworkers.
55. Help someone from out of town. Be an "ambassador" for your city.
56. Make your family's favorite dinner.
57. Offer someone a ride to an appointment or a store.
58. Open the door for another person.
59. Paint a picture for someone.
60. Pay for the dessert of an older couple in a restaurant.
61. Prepare a favorite meal or dish for a relative or friend.
62. Put some coins in someone else's parking meter.
63. Send someone a handwritten note of thanks.
64. Teach someone a new skill.
65. Thank a bus driver.
66. Visit a grandchild.
67. Bring homemade muffins or other treats to work.
68. Call, email, or write a note to a long-lost friend or relative.
69. Encourage others to talk about themselves and share.
70. Give an extra-big tip to someone.
71. Help rake your neighbor's leaves.
72. Make a card at home, and send it to a friend.
73. Offer to share your umbrella on a rainy day.
74. Say something nice about someone.

75. Send a personal thank-you note to someone who once helped you out.
76. Share a special memory with a friend or relative.
77. Visit a shut-in friend.
78. Welcome newcomers to a group.
79. Write a note of appreciation.
80. Write something nice about your waiter or waitress on the back of the bill.
81. Tell your children why you love them.
82. Be kind to yourself as well as to others.
83. Spend time with an elderly person. Find out some of his or her happiest memories.
84. Dedicate a song to someone.
85. Has a salesperson, waiter or waitress, or receptionist been pleasant and helpful? Send a note of commendation to his or her boss.
86. Hold the door of the elevator for someone trying to catch it.
87. Compliment someone on their clothing, on their hair, on their smile.
88. Help someone with an application or a resume.
89. Leave your neighbor a note saying how much you enjoy their garden.
90. Let a former teacher know how important he or she has been to you.

91. Let your friends and family know that you're always grateful. Have a "Thanksgiving" dinner in July.
92. Make a point of welcoming someone to your school or neighborhood.
93. Offer to look after a friend's or neighbor's pet.
94. Reconnect with a cousin or other relative.
95. Send a note to a role model—a teacher, perhaps, or a former neighbor—describing how he or she changed your life.
96. Send an old photograph to a friend, and explain what it means to you.
97. Send or bring flowers to a friend or neighbor.
98. Share your smile. You'll discover that smiling is contagious.
99. Take an older relative for a drive in the country.
100. Tell a coworker or neighbor how much you appreciate their style or attitude.
101. Think about someone you know who may be lonely—and bring some cheer his or her way.

PART TWO
Hope, Trust, and Faith

"For with God nothing will be impossible."
    —Luke 1:37

For I know the thoughts that I think toward you, says the Lord,
thoughts of peace and not of evil, to give you a future and a hope.
    —Jeremiah 29:11

It is good that one should hope and wait quietly
For the salvation of the Lord.
    —Lamentations 3:26

"Let not your heart be troubled; you believe in God, believe also
in Me."
    —John 14:1

. . . But he who trusts in the Lord, mercy shall surround him.
    —Psalm 32:10

Blessed is that man who makes the Lord his trust,
And does not respect the proud, nor such as turn aside to lies.
    —Psalm 40:4

For You are my hope, O Lord God;
You are my trust from my youth.
    —Psalm 71:5

Trust in the Lord with all your heart,
And lean not on your own understanding.
In all your ways acknowledge Him,
And He shall direct your paths.
—Proverbs 3:5–6

Whenever I am afraid,
I will trust in You.
In God (I will praise His word),
In God I have put my trust;
I will not fear.
What can flesh do to me?
—Psalm 56:3–4

And the apostles said to the Lord, "Increase our faith."
—Luke 17:5

So then faith comes by hearing, and hearing by the word of God.
—Romans 10:17

For by grace you have been saved through faith, and that not of
yourselves; it is the gift of God.
—Ephesians 2:8

Now faith is the substance of things hoped for, the evidence of
things not seen.
—Hebrews 11:1

NEVER BE AFRAID

Respect and trust—the two easiest things in life for someone to lose and the hardest things to get back.

—Unknown

A baby is God's opinion that the world should go on.

—Carl Sandburg

When I was young, my ambition was to be one of the people who made a difference in this world. My hope is to leave the world a little better for having been there.

—Jim Henson

How wonderful it is that nobody need wait a single moment before starting to improve the world.

—Anne Frank

Do not have your concert first, and then tune your instrument afterwards. Begin the day with the Word of God and prayer, and get first of all into harmony with Him.

—Hudson Taylor

Never be afraid to trust an unknown future to a known God.

—Corrie Ten Boom

What lies behind us and what lies ahead of us are tiny matters compared to what lies within us.

—Ralph Waldo Emerson (attrib.)

People are lonely because they build walls instead of bridges.

—Newton Joseph Fort

Carried through Grief

Roberta A. Neault

"Although God had put me back on my feet, He was still firmly holding my elbow as I regained my strength and took my first shaky steps."

"Footprints in the Sand" was my brother's favorite poem. I didn't know that until his spouse told me . . . the day we were planning his memorial. Sadly, this was one of many things we hadn't shared with each other. My father had always said we had more in common than we thought—and the fact that we both loved this poem was one more example of that.

Just weeks before my brother died, a new book in the Footprints collection had been published: *Footprints for Mothers and Daughters*. In it was a chapter I'd written—sadly, one more thing my brother and I hadn't talked about. Footprints author Margaret Fishback Powers, a dear friend, managed to gather together enough copies of the new book for me to give to my brother's spouse, stepchildren, and two nieces—my daughters— at his memorial service.

The following days were a dark, dark time in my life— exactly the times that the Footprints poem speaks to. I relied on God, and Gerry, my husband of thirty-four years, to carry me through. However, eight months later, just as I was starting to find a "new normal," my husband died tragically—essentially mid-conversation, so with no time at all to prepare. Once again, just as in "Footprints," God had to carry me through months of darkness. I began to really understand the impact of the "two becoming one"; when half of that one is ripped away, it's crippling and disorienting. I can't imagine walking that pathway without God in my life.

In our church in a small village outside of Vancouver, other members also suffered many tragic losses in the months after Gerry died. Knowing that my professional role involved teaching and motivational speaking, my pastor asked if I would share my story as a sermon one Sunday. I felt I was just barely surfacing at that point; to use the Footprints metaphor, although God had put me back on my feet, He was still firmly holding my elbow as I regained my strength and took my first shaky steps. Normally a confident presenter, I was unusually nervous about telling *this* story, worried that my emotions would take over and interfere with my ability to share what God wanted to say.

Once again, "Footprints" offered the solution. As I was preparing my message, I realized that much of my relevant story had been published in *Footprints for Mothers and Daughters* and, because "Footprints" is such a famous and well-loved poem, it would resonate with many people in the church. I chose to start my talk by reading *my* chapter, without mentioning until the end my connection to it. It was an effective way to share a complicated story without the emotional reactions that had worried me. Once again, God had picked me up and carried me. With the foundation in place, the rest of the talk flowed and accomplished exactly what the pastor had hoped it would, deeply touching many of the people in the congregation.

"Footprints" captures the essence of our faith—that we have a loving God to turn to in our darkest, weakest moments. He doesn't carry us just once but over and over again, whenever our own strength isn't enough to move us forward. The poem serves as a tangible reminder of a truth that we can hold on to in moments of deep loss and despair.

A Second Chance

Jody Bergsma

This story is by my artist friend, Jody. Although we know her well, we were never before aware of this story. Now I understand why she has been such a great friend to our family and such a positive influence on all of us.

This is a story about crisis, miracles, and God's love.

When I was a child, I died. I picked up a piece of bark near the fireplace and, as a kid would do, put it in my mouth. And then I choked.

As mayhem broke out and my parents wrestled with what was going on, my world began fading to black. And then it was gone.

My childhood was filled with the love of God. I remember singing "Jesus Loves Me" to our church congregation when I was just four, and I sang with gusto and faith. Happy days of stories from the Bible and a mother who showed me the all miracles of life gave me a rich beginning.

Who knows why tragedy strikes? Maybe it is because from crisis we learn about courage and overcoming adversity. Maybe that's when we learn the power of prayer. Mostly, I believe it's when we learn to have faith.

As darkness overcame me, I heard the words, "Jesus loves me, this I know." I felt a hand take mine. "For the Bible tells me so . . ." A light started to shine in the void. Maybe it was just my mother singing to me as we rushed twenty minutes to the hospital. Maybe the loving arms that held me were my parents' as they carried me into the emergency room.

Then the miracle came. That day, a renowned surgeon was visiting the hospital. As a specialist in blockages of the throat, he was called in and successfully removed the obstacle in my lungs. My lungs had collapsed, but I survived. I remained in the hospital for six weeks in an iron lung, forever remembering what had happened.

I never again feared death. I experienced something that I could not quite explain but that forever molded my faith and my life.

When I first read "Footprints in the Sand," I stopped, put my hands to my face, and cried. The poet had said it perfectly. I could see the sand. I remembered the arms. It was as if He were speaking the words to me, "It was then that I carried you." Jesus had carried me. The light was His eternal light, and the arms His own. My tragedy now had words.

Margaret Powers gave all of us a great gift in the poem "Footprints in the Sand." Millions of people, all facing personal challenges, drawbacks, handicaps, complications, difficulties, and problems have found reassurance in this inspired writing. What we did not know . . . became clear. When we felt abandoned . . . we learned we were not. When we felt weak . . . we remembered "He is strong."

In "Footprints," we hear the voice of God, saying

> *My precious child,*
> *I love you and will never leave you,*
> *never, ever, during your trials and testings.*
> *When you saw only one set of footprints,*
> *it was then that I carried you.*

I know it is true. It happened to me.

A Pair of Sandals

Dan Liebman

We search our minds to know what to say. Then we find the words in our hearts.

The most expensive pair of sandals I had ever bought—that's how I described them on the afternoon of July 23. On the morning of July 24, I called them the most precious pair I would ever own.

It was our friend Jean's birthday—her eightieth—and we were hosting a small dinner for her. We stopped to buy some flowers, and noticed that the shoe store next door was having a sale. I didn't need shoes, but what's that expression about a sale item? Something you never knew you needed till you discover that it's reduced by 50 percent. I bought the sandals—and the flowers—and we came home to put the finishing touches on dinner.

It promised to be quite a success. Jean and three of her close friends would arrive to a lovely table, a carefully planned menu, a pair of hosts who wanted to make the evening memorable, and Abby—the new arrival. Abby was a mutt, a mongrel, a mixture—we even called her a conundrum. (Once, when I walked Abby, a woman wanted to know "what kind of dog" she was. "A conundrum," I responded. "Oh," said the woman, "I never heard of that breed.") We had given her a "forever home" two months earlier, picking her up from her foster family. We couldn't resist the face on the Pet Rescue website, and soon we were filling out an elaborate application—fifteen pages! We were delighted to have passed the test.

We didn't know much about Abby, other than that she was four or a bit older, had had several litters of puppies, and had been rescued with her son Jack from a puppy mill in Kentucky and brought to Ontario by way of Ohio. We were told that she might have been bred so often so that she could nurse purebred pups. We were also told it could take a year or two for a rescue dog to begin feeling secure. That didn't matter. When we met her at the foster home, she charmed us. She was a "real" dog. And we fell in love with her deep brown eyes, which sparkled and hinted at some kind of mystery.

We spent the first two months getting to know each other. She had to play with every puppy she met on her walks. A few owners were intimidated because, although she wasn't a big dog—

twenty-five pounds, perhaps—she resembled a fox both in her coloring and in her features. But it never took them long to realize that all she wanted to do was to play. And she took an immediate liking to kids—the younger the better. We figured she wanted, or needed, to nurture little creatures. There were some difficult evenings. She had terrible nightmares, and we spent several nights comforting her and reassuring her that everything would be all right. Once somebody who was visiting set down a box, which must have reminded Abby of something dreadful. She growled and shook terribly.

We live in a tall apartment building and once, during Abby's first weeks with us, she and I were stuck in the elevator. She coped better than I did, and managed to calm (and charm) the three other occupants until a repairman rescued us an hour later.

Most of all, Abby made us laugh. She could entertain us for hours as she chased her tail, rolled over to be rubbed, brought us toys, or ignored us when she chose to. It didn't take long for us to realize she was the alpha in the family. We played with her when she wanted to play. If she wasn't in the mood, well, she ignored us. We called ourselves Abby's "butler" and "maid." We had no kids, and she brought laughter and warmth into our home.

She could be a little too friendly with visitors, and she was especially attentive to women. We think that, back in Kentucky, a woman had fed her and shown kindness. One of the first jobs on the training schedule was to get her to be less frisky. Other lessons would come later—some, we knew, she'd never learn. She pulled on her lead, though she was slightly more controlled when we used a harness. And she had no road sense. We lived beside an extended park, but there was a wide road—almost a highway—adjacent to our building.

On the evening of the dinner party, Jean and her friends—Marilyn, Joyce, and Jacquie—arrived at 6 p.m. Abby behaved splendidly. She was friendly and attentive, but not a pest. The meal was a success. Our friend Jean is fond of vegetables, and they were the theme of the evening—familiar vegetables served in unexpected ways. Dessert and coffee, a little chatting, and the four women headed home. It was nearly ten—a beautiful summer evening. The last vestiges of light had given way to darkness. It was time for Abby's last walk of the day.

I got her to step into her harness—she still wasn't used to it, and neither was I. But neighbors got a kick out of asking, "Is she walking you, or are you walking her?" With the harness, we hoped, I could answer that I was in charge.

Abby and I enjoyed a leisurely walk, stopping at her favorite places, and then headed home. As we approached the door to the building, I saw one of our neighbors—Mr. Young—head out with his pup, Chelsea. Mr. Young burst into a smile—he hadn't met Abby before. "Who do we have here?" he asked, as he bent down to pet her.

Then it happened in a flash. At that moment, just a few feet from the door, on an uneventful summer evening, feisty Abby wriggled out of her harness and took off into the night. Our little hound darted in front of me and ran toward the busy road.

I was in hot pursuit, but I was no match for the dog. At one point, she ran onto the road—but thankfully not into traffic. I raced beside her—this foxlike mutt running frantically, with a stream of cars behind her. And then, suddenly, I felt as if I was flying. My new pair of sandals had lifted me into the air—they gave me angel's wings. I had never moved at such a speed, and it was exhilarating.

After what seemed like miles but was likely a couple of blocks, Abby darted off the road and onto a muddy pathway beside it. She needed a rest and ran to a grassy area. I approached her and whispered her name. She took off. She stopped again. Leash and harness in hand, I once more whispered her name—and off she went. Then she stopped again. This time, I didn't move too close to her. "Abby," I whispered. She sat still. That was good. I would try a command. "Abby, come." She didn't move. "Abby, here," I said. Again, she sat still as I wondered if she'd again take off into the night. And then—I'm not sure why, but I was desperate—another phrase came into my mind: "Abby . . . *touch*!"

It worked. She came toward me, trustingly. She wasn't afraid. Quickly I clipped the leash to her collar.

⚘

WE WALKED HOME on the muddy path that ran alongside the road. Only then did I realize how exhausted I was, not just from racing down the road but also from the thought that I could have lost this precious new friend forever. Here and there, I saw Abby's fresh paw prints as well as the prints from my new sandals.

One set of each.

Sometimes I Walk on Water

Michelle Holmes

"I found myself not desperately seeking a miracle but quietly standing in the very presence of the Healer."

Redeemed, redeemed, redeemed. The words came rushing up from the pit of my stomach and exploded through my mouth. I found myself anointing my forehead with oil as I stared at my grief-stricken reflection in the bathroom mirror.

Just two hours earlier, I had heard the awful words that every woman dreads: "The biopsy results are back. It is malignant. You will have to undergo a mastectomy." After my plethora of questions, and when the doctor's words had finally sunk in, I put the phone down and sobbed and sobbed. The very word *cancer* brought with it thoughts of death. I had lost my mother and aunt to the same deadly disease.

Redeemed, redeemed, redeemed. I was in shock and numb with fear as I stood in front of the mirror a few hours later, so I knew that those powerful words of redemption had come from somewhere other than this "faith-filled woman" (as I classified myself).

At that moment, I in no way *felt* anything other than scared, weepy, and very, very alone.

During the days and weeks and months that followed, I did turn to God. I prayed, pleaded, begged, and cajoled, and silently stood in faith believing for a miracle. I promised Him I would help every other woman on the planet; I would tell everyone in every church about what He had done for me; the doctors would be amazed and it would be such a wonderful story to bring glory to His name. I read testimonials of miraculous healings; I watched every Christian television program I could find. I read the Word constantly. I prayed alone and with others and I believed, oh how I believed, that my faith would move this mountain. But as the chemotherapy treatments took their toll and the surgery date loomed closer and closer, the miracle I was waiting for did not come.

To say I was disappointed and discouraged and so full of questions about God not coming through for me in the way I expected would be an understatement. Although I had believed in a miracle-working God and believed Jesus still heals today, I was now at a crossroads in my faith in this particular area. Friends were telling me about yoga and other coping mechanisms that they used. So how could I tell them about a powerful, miracle-working God who was keeping so silent when I expected him to come through? The thing was, I had seen God work in my life before, and I knew how He had come through for me in desperate times; how He had lifted and carried me when I could barely place one foot in front of the other; and how faithful He had always been through very uncertain and rocky times. Jesus had always been my anchor, and the Holy Spirit had always led me through shaky territory. But now, when it came to my health, this was a totally different ball game. My faith was precariously clinging to the hem of His garment. So that's where I was—despondent, dejected, and without hope, wondering why God was silent, why He wasn't answering me in the way I expected, and why His time frame was so different to mine.

One morning in His ever-gentle way, as I was mulling over the question of healing, God showed me that He is sovereign, and I found myself not desperately seeking a miracle but quietly standing in the very presence of the Healer. That was it. God had been with me all along. As I thought about the most painful times when I felt I just couldn't take one more chemotherapy treatment because of the ravaging side effects, I was reminded of the beautiful poem my mother had given me long ago, and it dawned on me that I had been carried. I wasn't going *around* this awful experience, but I was going *through* it, and I wasn't alone.

Just before the extensive ten-hour surgery, I opened my Bible and read these words:

Fear not (Michelle), for I have redeemed you;
I have called you by your name;
You are Mine.
When you pass through the waters, I will be with you;
And through the rivers, they shall not overflow you.
When you walk through the fire, you shall not be burned,
Nor shall the flame scorch you.
For I am the Lord your God
  —Isaiah 43:1–3

As the operating room doors were swinging shut, I glanced back, and I could swear I saw a set of footprints—just one set. God had answered my prayers—perhaps not in the way I had expected Him to, but there was no denying it. I had my miracle.

I'm Not Alone

George Schmidt

When things appear hopeless, we find something—a book, a poem, a message from a loved one—that reminds us we are not alone.

My dad passed away when I was sixteen, fifty years ago. I was the youngest child, and when Dad became ill, my older brother was at college and my sister was married. Mom was at work. So, for many days during Dad's last months in the hospital, it was just the two of us. When he was feeling up to it, Dad and I would go for a walk. I didn't realize it then, but he used these walks to pass along important life lessons. He did so in a gentle, nonjudgmental way, and only later did I realize that he was directing these lessons at me. "A person should think before speaking," he'd tell me, for example. Only years later, when I said something that I instantly regretted as the words left my mouth, did I realize that I was the person Dad had in mind. He also taught me by example.

My mom passed away a few years ago. She was just over ninety years old. Although she lived a full, rich life, her death was a difficult loss for me. I think I inherited her sense of humor and her sense of curiosity. Mom was always acutely aware of her surroundings—if I moved a picture on the wall, ever so slightly, she'd immediately notice. And she loved words and numbers. Something as seemingly ordinary as the time of day intrigued her. She'd point to the digital clock when it read 11:11 or 12:34. Along the same lines, she'd always find something special in people—children especially—that others just wouldn't notice.

For the past year, I've been going through a difficult time. My health has suffered, a friendship has ended on an unhappy note, and my job has become increasingly stressful. I try to focus on the good in life, and I find it helps to reread favorite books from my childhood. I have also found tremendous comfort in the message of the poem "Footprints in the Sand," which reminds me that I do not have to face my challenges on my own.

I've noticed that when I'm at a particularly low point, a light on my dashboard starts to flicker for a few seconds while I'm driving. I spoke to my mechanic about it and he says it's nothing to worry about—it's a short in the electrical system and isn't worth the bother of fixing. But there's a definite trend. I feel anxious or upset, and at that point, the little light starts flickering. At first I thought it was strange, but I've come to believe it's my dad giving me a sign that things will get better. Other times, when I feel discouraged, my eyes move to the clock on the radio. I'm sure it's no coincidence that, so many times, the clock reads 12:34. That makes me smile, helps brighten the moment, and, rather than focus on my despair, I count my many blessings and think about a brighter future.

The Three Bells

Steve Connolly

This story by our friend Steve is about recovery, God's grace and guidance, and what it truly means to celebrate life.

I was a twenty-four-year-old engineer working for one of Canada's first high-tech companies in Ottawa in 1967. I was single and loved to party. My friends and I celebrated life almost every night in the pubs and clubs across the river, at embassy functions, in our apartment, and elsewhere. I was also setting records for working overtime at my company, building computer systems for the military. I needed the loot to pay for my new 1966 all-white Mustang convertible.

On Labor Day weekend that year, I traveled with four girl-friends to the beautiful beaches of Grand Bend on Lake Huron for some hilarious partying. No end of fun.

On returning to Ottawa, I began to feel anxious and uneasy. I didn't know why. It wouldn't stop—and neither did my partying, or my working overtime. My anxiety worsened, and I visited a doctor who diagnosed me as being mildly depressed. *Me?* Mildly depressed? I could not believe what I had heard, and I refused to accept it.

My physical and mental situation gradually became worse until one evening, I had to ask my beautiful new girlfriend, Carolyn, to come to my shared apartment to help me, even though I did not know what was bothering me. I was terribly anxious and nervous. All my life I had been highly athletic, had met my academic challenges, and had been a confident achiever. I was losing confidence in myself for no evident reason.

A few evenings later, while being comforted by relatives of Carolyn, I reached a peak of nervousness and illness and was taken by ambulance to the psychiatric ward of the Ottawa Hospital. I was given a shot of medicine to relax me. I was having a nervous breakdown—something that other people had, but never, I thought, would happen to me. I remained in the ward for two weeks, with other patients in terrible shape. Some were suicidal; one often talked loudly on the telephone, with nobody on the other end; and many were rolled out in the early mornings to have electric shock treatment.

The only thing that I enjoyed about all of this was making baskets out of Popsicle sticks in the afternoons with some of the other patients. My parents traveled from their home in Kitimat,

British Columbia, where I had been mostly raised, to Ottawa—hugely concerned about their oldest son in his incomprehensible predicament. None of us had any answers, and remaining in the depressing hospital environment—guided by an unfeeling doctor—was not going to help.

We tried for two weeks to set me up in a furnished apartment to keep me away from my own apartment, which, although shared with two great friends, was not the environment I needed for my recovery. That did not work. In December, my family and I decided I should fly home to Kitimat and stay with my caring and perfect parents. Nothing in the world could provide me with a better place to deal with my recovery from an illness that I did not understand than this home full of the objects, family, and memories of my wonderful youth.

My special Carolyn visited for Christmas. What a blessing. She always recalls this special time when she met so many wonderful people and took in the beauty of the surrounding mountains and the huge snowfalls that descended on us that year. She was precious to me in my condition, but she had to return to her work in Ottawa. I was still at the lowest-ever point in my life.

Everyone was concerned for me. At the time, my father was a top engineer working for a major Canadian corporation. All his life he had been a "can-do," problem-solving type of person. He would tell my younger brother and me that, at six months of age, he had crawled all the way by himself to a baby show, where he won a blue ribbon. Yet here he was, confronted with his son crying on the floor at his feet and, for once in his life, he did not know what to do.

One morning, my mother proposed that she and I go to the Christ the King Catholic Church to pray for my recovery. My father had helped to build this church. I agreed, and we found ourselves kneeling all alone in front of the altar on which my brother and I had served as altar boys years before.

During my illness, I had never lost my faith in God and had prayed every day. In the church, beside my wonderful mother, I prayed again for help. I knew that the good times I had known would return again, but I also realized that I was up against a really tough challenge. For this, I would need God's help. I knew that this was the worst time of my life, but that there was a purpose to it, and that it might also be the best time of my life because I might learn from it and become a better, more capable person. Yet, how must I proceed?

As we were kneeling, the parish priest approached us and my mother introduced me to him. He must have known of my situation since, after some initial discussion, he offered me the opportunity to teach in the St. Anthony's Catholic School with no strings attached, no pay, for as long as I wanted and to teach any subjects that I wanted. That evening, my mother pressed for me to accept the offer, although in my condition, I just wanted to say at home, eat her puddings, and wait for a miracle to happen.

Fortunately, I chose to accept. I began to teach math, chemistry, and physical education. The process of teaching the receptive youngsters began to bring back some of my confidence. It relieved me of my focus on my illness to some extent. I actually began to enjoy it. I continued to pray for God's help.

One day, the priest invited me over to his house to meet some new friends and to socialize. For the first time, I listened to the beautiful music of the song "The Three Bells," and the story of little Jimmy Brown. I felt at peace with myself in this comforting environment. I did not know it then, but I would always remember this song and this time.

A few days later, my capable father suggested to me that I talk to an engineer friend of his who had suffered a nervous breakdown some years previously and had successfully recovered. The next Sunday afternoon, Mr. Thompson sat alone with me in our family living room and listened to my story intently without interruption. He was a capable, quiet, and calm individual.

It was at this time that my terrible decline in health began its turn upward. The pain in my mind was excruciating. I would have suffered the cutting off of an arm without a painkiller if doing so would have ended my mental pain. Mr. Thompson told me that the solution to my problem, in his opinion, was not medication—as I had felt it would be. He stated that my brain was confused. In Ottawa, I had not been behaving in a way that was true to myself. Trying to be the life of the party was not my real self. I needed to review my actions, simplify my life, and get back to *my* normal behavior.

Not long afterward, I returned to Ottawa to stay with a wonderful family who were close friends of my parents. Their place became a second home for me, where I was comforted in a quiet, intelligent, and reassuring environment. It worked. I returned to my job, where management had been tremendously accommodating of my situation. I stopped putting in overtime, for the most part, and stopped the partying. My great girlfriend, Carolyn, and her Irish farming family in the Gatineau Hills played a huge positive role in my recovery.

In August 1968, Carolyn and I were married. I recovered fully and became an even more capable person and, certainly, a better one. We have raised two talented children and are blessed with five also-special grandchildren.

I still believe that this experience was the best of my life. I learned greatly from it. Some forty-five years later, I was able to locate a delighted Mr. Thompson to thank him profusely for his help.

At the crux of the solution to my illness was my real and deep faith in God. As in the final words of the renowned poem "Footprints in the Sand," He had carried me when I most needed help. When I listen again to "The Three Bells," I know that He was all three bells for me.

Do Not Fear, I Am with You

Joy Gove

"My greatest worry was that I would lose my sense of joy to a sense of fear, and I knew my only protection against that was to remain very close to God, with an attitude of praise and thanksgiving."

It was October 2005—two months after I had felt a lump in my right breast. My doctor had told me in August that it was nothing, but suggested I go for a mammogram because it had been some time since I had had one.

I took my time making an appointment, but when I was given a date off in the distance, something inside of me panicked. *Six weeks was too long to wait!* In just a couple of weeks, I had noticed the lump had grown to the size of an egg, and I knew I'd better get it checked out sooner rather than later.

Nonetheless, I didn't tell anyone other than my husband, in the hope that all this was just a bad dream. I was able to get in to see the doctor and start the process in just a few days, but my test results were inconclusive and I would need more tests.

Before I went for my biopsies, a friend told me that you could ask the technician how things looked, and he'd generally tell you. So I did that—but I didn't hear the news I was hoping for. He told me he was concerned and that it didn't look good. I knew in my heart that I probably had breast cancer.

What do I do now? Do I tell my friends? Do I tell my family? What if he is wrong? My mind was racing with all the what-ifs.

The next ten days felt like an eternity. Finally, on day ten, I decided to phone my doctor for the results. To my utter amazement, the technician had been wrong—the tests came back benign! I was absolutely elated. I celebrated on the weekend but made an appointment with my physician for the following Monday, because I still needed to know what that "egg" was, if it wasn't cancer.

I arrived at my doctor's office excited and still in a state of happy shock, and was able to share my excitement with a friend who happened to be in the waiting area because she had an appointment with the doctor right after mine. My friend was a nurse at the British Columbia Cancer Agency. She had a benign tumor in her breast and was scheduled to see her surgeon the following day.

I entered my doctor's office proclaiming with excitement, "Isn't that wonderful there is no cancer!" only to hear, "Well, actually, a second report has come in and it *is* cancer." Bewildered and shaken, I still had the presence of mind to bring in my friend from the waiting room, recognizing that there was a good chance I would not comprehend anything I was about to be told.

God had arranged this appointment long beforehand, since my friend not only was there to support me, but also generously relinquished her appointment for the following day and gave it to me. Within twenty-four hours of hearing the news, I was in the surgeon's office receiving the protocol that would last an entire year. I was going to need surgery, chemotherapy, and radiation. I felt shell-shocked, and my husband nearly fainted on the spot.

Two days later I returned to work and was greeted by a client with a big bouquet of flowers—for no apparent reason—but God knew the reason: I needed to be reminded that He was in control, and that He would be with me on the journey ahead. I kept track throughout my journey of times when God blessed me and reassured me through acts of kindness of others, and it served as great encouragement to me.

Very soon after I was given my diagnosis and course of treatment, I knew I had to make a firm commitment to myself to do whatever it took to guard my heart and mind, and fill it with the truth from Scripture so that my heart would know that God was my rock and my salvation and that I would not be shaken. My greatest worry was that I would lose my sense of joy to a sense of fear, and I knew my only protection against that was to remain very close to God, with an attitude of praise and thanksgiving. His Word says that He inhabits the praises of His people.

I believed in my heart that God would miraculously heal me and that I wouldn't have to go through all the treatments, but that was not meant to be. Nonetheless, with Proverbs 3:5–6 ("Trust in the Lord with all your heart, And lean not on your own understanding"), I continued to trust Him and enjoy His presence. I was to learn that, in trusting God, the real freedom wasn't necessarily in trusting that all would go the way I wanted it to go, but in trusting that He was sovereign and in control and that He loved me and would be with me no matter what.

I immersed myself in Scripture and good Christian teaching throughout that year. It was a wonderful start to the realization that God means what He says in the Word. God had always been very important in my life, but He was taking me to a deeper level with Him. If He wasn't faithful, I was hooped!

The Lord provided me with a strong support network in my loving husband, family, and friends. I felt very loved and cared for. I made sure I kept my sense of humor and arranged for enjoyable outings whenever I could. I bought the cutest wig I could find and had fun with it. I even wore barrettes in it so people wouldn't realize it was a wig—and they didn't.

I treated myself to whatever struck my fancy on a fairly regular basis. I celebrated each landmark with something to look forward to. For example, at the halfway point of my chemo treatments, my husband and I went away for a weekend with an outdoor bathtub right along the ocean. So I smothered myself in bubbles and enjoyed the sunset—bald head and all!

Sometimes when fear crept into my heart, my husband would remind me of Psalm 139:16: "Your eyes saw my substance, being yet unformed. And in Your book they all were written, The days fashioned for me, when as yet there were none of them."

John Piper, a theologian and preacher, went through prostate cancer at the same time as I was going through my breast cancer. He preached a sermon that he entitled, "Don't Waste Your Cancer." He challenged me to use my cancer experience to bring glory to God through trusting Him and sharing with others how He was my strength.

In turn, I hope that the story of my journey through breast cancer will be helpful to others facing challenges—not only challenges related to cancer.

Through Happiness and Sorrows

Joyce Bilton

"Perhaps you, too, have sensed that feeling of being carried when the going gets tough."

My story begins with what the imagery in the poem means to me.

As I walk in my life, God is by my side. He holds my hand through every circumstance—sunny, refreshing days and dark ones; untroubled nights, or long, stormy ones. During the good times, as we walk side by side, I sense Him near me. There are two sets of footprints, side by side. Then, during the disturbing hours, He draws me to Him and carries me in His arms, and there is peace.

This knowledge is in the deepest recesses of my heart. No matter what may come my way, I feel comforted in His presence. We communicate through prayer, song, and His given word, spoken and unspoken. There is rest and serenity in the assurance that He has my complete life in His hands. As I reflect on the lines of this poem, many scenes of my life come to mind.

I remember when I was about eleven and a half years old and very ill with rheumatic fever. This was during the Second World War, before antibiotics were available. At the time, we were living in four small rooms partitioned off at the end of a long chicken house. The doctor stood in the doorway and advised my mother to get my father home from wherever he was stationed. He did not think I would last the weekend. I vaguely remember my father being present at some point. My mother was holding me. Three days later, I woke up. The fever had broken.

At age eighteen I found my faith, which would change my life and actions. A few years later it was tested when I was aboard a ship in a terrible storm in the Pacific Northwest, off the coast of Oregon and Washington State. The captain and crew were sure we were going down and prepared the passengers for the worst. During an interview, after we had finally reached Vancouver, British Columbia, the captain said that it had been the worst storm he had ever experienced in his twenty-nine years sailing the Pacific Ocean. I was not afraid. I sensed the Lord was carrying me.

Several years later I was living in Portland, Oregon. On a very dark and rainy night, I was about to park a company station wagon. I saw nothing behind me but suddenly found myself flying through the air. I had no idea what had happened, but was later told that a car with its lights off had rear-ended me. The driver was drunk and was speeding, and had neither license nor insurance. The station wagon was thrust about forty feet down the road and then over a curb, the front end hitting a pole. The driver was arrested that night, bailed out the next morning, and disappeared. I was severely injured, with a broken neck—among other injuries. The doctor said it was a miracle that I had survived. Once again the Lord carried me in His arms.

Early on Christmas morning 1954, while living in southern California, I had a beautiful experience. The previous evening had been mild, and I had left the window open. I woke to the sound of heavenly singing. I got out of bed and knelt by the open window, wondering who was out at that time singing Christmas carols. I was awake and not dreaming. In the predawn morning I heard angelic voices singing "Hark! The Herald Angels Sing."

Over the years, the Lord has carried me through happiness and sorrows, through good times and troubled times. That is why the poem "Footprints in the Sand" is so personal and real to me. It was also precious to my mother, and was read at her memorial service. Perhaps you, too, have sensed that feeling of being carried when the going gets too tough.

Carried as on the Wings of an Eagle

Lesley Anthea Lewis

"There is no time limit attached to how long the Lord is willing to carry us."

The poem "Footprints in the Sand" shocked me when I first read it. I recognized that the two sets of footprints disappeared, and then became one. Where did God go? I assumed that He had disappeared and left the person alone. Because of my personal life I have walked alone a lot, and so, on reading the poem, I felt that the person was left to figure things out on his or her own.

My father was a card-carrying atheist. He rebelled and left his childhood religion when he was young. With his freethinker's pride, he passed on his beliefs to the five children he reared. My mother needed to work and be independent and avoided being with us, her own children. My childhood years were spent with numerous strangers, and I firmly believe that God had pre-arranged for them to care for me. Most of the caregivers were wonderful. They included many different housekeepers, new friends, relatives, and neighbors. Some I still miss deeply.

When I was five, one cleaning woman went over my father's authority, and taught my sisters and me that there was a God to pray to, and that He listened. It was a profound lesson for me. My sisters, however, did not like to pray, and they rejected her ideas. The woman was soon asked to leave.

In my innocence of faith, I started to look for Jesus in others. When I was in eighth grade, my mother, her current boyfriend, my four-year-old twin brothers, and I were secretly taken to relatives to hide from my dad for six months. We would live together for many years at our summer cottage home at Edmonton Beach. A totally new life began for us. We loved our dad, but he was allowed to visit only occasionally. My mother wanted to start her "new" life without our dad in it, and that decision broke our hearts.

Our cottage was converted into a place of both beauty and horror. It had propane heating, no running water, and outdoor plumbing. We would gratefully receive meager bags of groceries and various treats from my mother's boyfriends and, occasionally, from friends. I grew physically very strong from carrying buckets of water from the well and from the many walks that I took alone up the roads and through the fields. How God protected me!

Finally one summer, with our larder reduced to a box of corn-flakes that housed a large moth, my mother became desperate and we went on welfare. For years, we rode the school bus daily to a small town school, where I met wonderful Christian people. Events in our school and town hall included prayers and carols at Christmas. I spent time with children raised in loving homes. My faith grew stronger as I witnessed God's protection of my brothers and me. Somehow I knew I was never alone.

Approximately one month before my brothers' twelfth birthday, my mother had married Ken, a Yellowknife federal worker. Realizing that I needed to do something for myself, God led me to a safe environment—a nursing school. The Royal Alexandra School of Nursing offered three years of free room and board. I felt comfortable leaving home, knowing my brothers now had a kindly man to be a father to them. I had always prayed that they would have a father before they reached the age of twelve. Sadly, Ken died three years later.

During my training, in the late 1960s, I was known as a fun-loving person, but God kept me from going too far, too fast. I met my husband at a nurses' dance. We were married about six months after I graduated. From almost the beginning, our marriage was in trouble, but I learned to lean on the Lord. My husband and I stayed married about thirty-eight years, and we raised three children.

In my troubled marriage, I transitioned from a life of walking with the Lord to being carried by him, many times. The decay of our marriage became slowly and painfully obvious, until our divorce was finalized. I felt ashamed that I could not keep our marriage together. My family, my church, and my God meant so much to me. The final act of the marriage breakdown produced a sense of loss, guilt, and rejection. The turmoil tore me up both emotionally and spiritually. The unseen branding with a scarlet letter of divorce was never my goal. I yearned for a family of joy and peace.

While at Bible camp with my children, I had the pleasure of meeting Paul and Margaret Powers. Margaret's sweet, humble spirit amazed me as she assisted Paul with his puppets and taught and sang with the children at camp. Again God carried me through those years, tears, and triumphs. I went on to become a camp chapel speaker and teacher for ten years. I used the Powers' suggestions and examples on how to lead children toward the Word of God.

I can't emphasize enough the importance of the "Footprints" poem to me: it led me to the moment when I realized who was carrying whom. The Lord had found me and lifted me up in His arms, gently and safely. I was reclining in His safe arms. He held me with firm kindness through rough and stormy paths that I could not have predicted.

I also discovered through the poem that there is no time limit attached to how long the Lord is willing to carry me. He understands when I am carrying a heavy load and my steps are not strong. There was a time when I thought I was ready for a new life and wanted to jump down from His arms and fix my own problems, but He lovingly continued to carry me and knew exactly when I was ready to place my new set of footprints beside His.

Looking back, I reflect on my beautiful home where we raised the children. Now, a new family is raising their children there. Once I dropped in to visit and saw that the owners had mounted a plaque with words of Scripture on one of the pillars at the front of the house. It read, "I am the vine, you are the branches" (John 15:5). That pleased me so much.

I followed my children and grandchildren to a new city, a new home, and a new church. Strangers now greet me on Sundays as I walk in, seemingly alone. I may be taking new steps, but I am never alone. It thrills me to imagine walking with the Lord and sharing my new path on the road.

My footprints do not resemble my previous ones. My feet are older, I walk more slowly, and I still stumble at times. His footprints remain steady and mark the way as He shows me my new path.

PART THREE
Burdens, Courage, and Strength

Be of good courage,
And He shall strengthen your heart,
All you who hope in the Lord.
    —Psalm 31:24

Fear not, for I am with you;
Be not dismayed, for I am your God.
I will strengthen you,
Yes, I will help you,
I will uphold you with My righteous right hand.
    —Isaiah 41:10

Cast your burden on the Lord,
And He shall sustain you;
He shall never permit the righteous to be moved.
    —Psalm 55:22

"Come to Me, all you who labor and are heavy laden, and I will
    give you rest.
Take My yoke upon you and learn from Me, for I am gentle and
    lowly in heart, and you will find rest in your souls.
For My yoke is easy and My burden is light."
    —Matthew 11:28–30

Bear one another's burdens, and so fulfill the law of Christ.
    —Galatians 6:2

Finally, my brethren, be strong in the Lord and in the power of His might.
—Ephesians 6:10

God is our refuge and strength,
A very present help in trouble.
—Psalm 46:1

O Lord, my strength and my fortress,
My refuge in the day of affliction . . .
—Jeremiah 16:19

THE WEIGHT OF ANOTHER'S BURDEN

No one is useless in this world who lightens the burden of it to anyone else.

—Charles Dickens

Any concern too small to be turned into a prayer is too small to be made into a burden.

—Corrie Ten Boom

None knows the weight of another's burden.

—George Herbert

God places the heaviest burden on those who can carry its weight.

—Reggie White

Some people will always throw stones in your path. It depends on what you make with them—a bridge or a wall. Remember, you are the architect of your life.

—Unknown

The shortest answer is doing.

—George Herbert

If God sends us on strong paths, He provides strong shoes.

—Corrie Ten Boom

With courage you will dare to take risks, have the strength to be compassionate, and the wisdom to be humble. Courage is the foundation of integrity.

—Mark Twain

Storms make the oak grow deeper roots.

—George Herbert

Courage is what it takes to stand up and speak; courage is also what it takes to sit down and listen.

—Winston Churchill

Another Day

Faye Dewhurst

Last year, my friend Faye Dewhurst expressed her feelings, and her faith, in anticipation of her chemotherapy treatment for cancer. Faye recently passed away, but I believe the words she wrote will convey the exceptional dignity and grace with which she faced her illness. I hope they will provide strength to others. This is an excerpt from her writings.

> *He will feed His flock like a shepherd;*
> *He will gather the lambs with His arm,*
> *And carry them in His bosom,*
> *And gently lead those who are with young.*
> *—Isaiah 40:11*

When we are struggling through the ravages of cancer, we wonder if our painful existence has a reason. And the nights, oh the long dark nights we spend wrestling with unanswered questions and feelings of abandonment and wondering if we will have the strength to make it through another day. But we were never meant to walk this road alone, for God has promised to walk it with us.

The next few months of anticipated discomfort and loneliness are just that, anticipated, but I know that God has promised to supply the strength, the breath, and the divine stamina to endure each day as I lean on Him. He will carry me and be my strength to pull me through each long treatment. He will reach for me and take my hand and pray with me. We will stand together and be strong. And when there are times when I'm too weak to drive forward for another day, He will carry me.

Whatever encumbrances weigh us down and cause our minds to welcome death, this is when, at our weakest state, God will provide the strength.

"No temptation has overtaken you except such as is common to man; but God is faithful, who will not allow you to be tempted beyond what you are able, but with the temptation will also make the way of escape, that you may be able to bear it" (1 Corinthians 10:13).

The Shrouded Moon

Marilyn Stremler

"Some life experiences appear so ordinary yet are so sacred that one initially fails to grasp their momentous import."

July 14, 1996, is indelibly etched in our memory. As my husband and I enjoyed the cool evening air on our patio after a hot day in the Pacific Northwest, we heard the sound of a police siren. As was my habit, I prayed for the "unknown" people needing emergency help. Minutes later, our telephone rang. The caller informed us that our second son, Jeff, had fallen from his horse in a field nearby and was injured. We rushed to the scene and found Jeff lying on the ground, surrounded by paramedics. I kneeled where I could touch his leg and began praying. Minutes later, he was put on a gurney and loaded into the ambulance. I asked if I could ride with him and was instructed to sit in the front with the driver. All the way to the local hospital I prayed, asking God to spare Jeff's life. We hadn't a clue about the extent of Jeff's injuries but knew, because he had not regained consciousness, that they could be serious.

A few days later, we learned Jeff had sustained traumatic brain injury: a left-brain injury and a brain-stem injury. No, we didn't initially know what all this entailed. But, yes, we knew a few people who had sustained brain injuries. We knew about their outcomes, but we were convinced that God had other plans for Jeff.

Fast forward a few months. After three weeks in the critical-care unit and a week in another ward, Jeff was transferred to our local long-term-care facility. His eyes had opened on the fifteenth day. However, it was apparent that he was not aware of his environment. Very slowly he began to respond to simple commands. "Catch the ball, Jeff." "Put your hat on, Jeff." "It's time to get out of the car, Jeff."

Even though he was wheelchair-bound, non-verbal, and barely able to hold his head up, we decided to start taking him home for our dinner hour, hoping that being in a familiar environment would help him to regain awareness sooner. Exposure to the sounds and smells of home seemed to calm and comfort him. The schedule of days at the care center and evenings in our home with Jeff brought some structure to a maze of days and months that otherwise had few rituals or routines. However, returning to the care center at nine in the evening was a painful struggle. Each night, when it was time to transfer him from the car to his wheelchair, Jeff planted his foot on the floorboard and would not budge. Using the only means of communication he could, he was emphatically telling us, "I do not want to go back to Room 102." Only after much coaxing and cajoling would he cooperate and allow me to help him return to his room.

One evening as I was driving Jeff back to the care center, I felt particularly sad. On arrival, once again the foot was firmly planted and it seemed no amount of talking would change his mind. I was helpless to move him unless he cooperated. Getting chilled in the wet, windy, cold weather, I finally told Jeff that I was going inside the front doors and I would come out soon to see if he was ready. A bit later, close to tears, I was able to convince Jeff that we needed to get him into the wheelchair, and tearfully I left him once more.

Driving the ten blocks home, I cried out to God, "I'd like to plant my foot as well, Lord. This is not what I bargained for either." Several thoughts flooded my mind: *"I will never leave you nor forsake you." "Trust in the Lord with all your heart." "God is our refuge and our strength."* These were verses I had memorized as a child. As I scanned the dark autumn sky, I noticed the moon. Its bright, full face, shrouded by a dark mass of clouds, seemed to demand my attention. Almost the entire moon was darkened by the clouds passing over it. This was, I suddenly realized, an image of Jeff's condition. His brain had been so clouded over by the devastating injury. I then noticed the changing configuration of the clouds. They were moving slowly, allowing more of the moon's bright light to be exposed. As I rounded the bend on Front Street, I could no longer see the moon but felt an urgency to watch the progression from dark to light. I sped home, where I'd be able to view the moon once more. Hurrying to the backyard, I saw that most of the clouds had cleared the face of the moon. Only a small residue remained. As sure as the promise of a rainbow, I perceived this sign from nature as a promise from God: "Jeff's mind will not always be as clouded as it is now. The darkness and confusion will pass, although a small residue will remain." I wept and was comforted.

The process is long and arduous and, as we walk this path, God takes our hand and walks with us. When the journey is the hardest, we feel God carrying us. My friend Margaret Powers's poem "Footprints in the Sand" is a constant source of comfort. For Jeff, these words are particularly meaningful as he lives with his disability:

> . . . *"My precious child,*
> *I love you and will never leave you,*
> *never, ever, during your trials and testings,*
> *When you saw only one set of footprints,*
> *it was then that I carried you."*

Today, much of the shrouding of Jeff's mind has been cleared. We await the day when he will be whole, body and mind, with the Lord.

Talking to the Children

Sylvia Bosworth

When a friend found the courage to speak out, she turned a heartbreaking experience into a life-changing opportunity.

I don't know if Roberta Jones ever read "Footprints in the Sand," the inspirational poem that has enriched so many lives. But when I think of the poem's words—"My precious child, I love you and will never leave you"—I think of Roberta.

Roberta's ancestors arrived in Canada through the Underground Railroad—the network of secret routes used by black slaves to escape to "free" states and to Canada. They settled near Barrie, Ontario—farm country north of Toronto. Roberta would have been born about 1930. She sometimes talked about her childhood on the family farm, always with affection and respect for her hard-working family and neighbors. A few years before she passed away, I helped Roberta find some of the census records dating from her childhood. In the records, members of the black community were identified as "colored," and as Roberta recognized the name of a neighbor, she'd comment, "That person was good to our family." Or she'd say nothing.

At some point, she left the farm and moved to Toronto, marrying and raising her family. Then the marriage fell apart, and she needed to find work outside the home. She took a job cleaning for my friend Marilyn, and the two women became fast friends and found they had a number of common interests, including a love of history.

One morning, as Roberta was walking from her bus stop to Marilyn's home, a school bus drove past her. A couple of students pushed their heads out of the window and hurled racial slurs at her.

I think that's when she felt abandoned and alone. Her ancestors had been slaves but escaped to freedom—and a chance for their children, and children's children, to have new opportunities. She had to leave school early to help on the farm. Her marriage had ended in disaster. And now she was hurt deeply by ugly words. Where was the opportunity her family had hoped for?

Marilyn, who hadn't yet left for work when Roberta walked in that morning, knew something was terribly wrong. Over a cup of coffee, Roberta shared what had happened. Marilyn was outraged and asked her friend if she knew what school the children attended. She did—it was a grade school between Roberta's own bus stop and Marilyn's house.

"Roberta," Marilyn said to her. "I'm going to call the principal of the school and let him know those children should be disciplined."

"No," Roberta said. "Let me make the call."

⁜

ROBERTA REACHED THE PRINCIPAL THAT DAY, and they had a long conversation. The principal said he could find out who the students were. He could punish them, but he could also educate them. Would Roberta help?

"Mrs. Jones," he said to her. "I'd like you to speak to my classes. Tell them how you felt when you heard those hurtful words this morning."

When Marilyn came home that day, she was surprised to see that Roberta was still there. Where Roberta's eyes looked sad earlier in the day, they now sparkled.

"I spoke to the school principal," Roberta said with a mixture of excitement and nervousness. "Next week, I will be talking to an assembly at his school."

⁜

WHAT DID ROBERTA SAY to her audience of several hundred youngsters who gathered in the school auditorium that day? I don't know. But she had such an effect on them that soon another school in the district asked her to speak to its students. Then another school asked her to speak—and then another one.

She continued to speak to schools and eventually enrolled at university and fulfilled her life's dream of getting a degree—a master's degree—in education. At the time of her death, she had been a guidance counselor for many years, working in one of the city's toughest schools.

Outwardly, she cut her students little slack when they said they'd been dealt a bad hand in life. But although she took no "guff" from her kids, she fought for them every day. And she inspired an untold number of young people to better their lives, as she had bettered hers.

Waiting for the Streetcar

Linda Dee Smith

Sometimes we see only what we want to see . . . or what we choose to see.

He was sitting on the bench at the streetcar stop in front of St. Joseph's Hospital, a slightly bedraggled middle-aged man. Nearby was a shopping buggy, filled with what I imagined were all his worldly goods. She was sitting beside him, dressed in a pantsuit, her hair blowing in the early autumn breeze as she spoke animatedly to him. A backpack was placed on the bench between the two of them. I was among the other people waiting for the long-overdue streetcar, and I found myself listening in on their conversation. It was a mild evening, and you could hear the rustle of the wind in the trees in the park to our west.

He was telling her about his recent experience in the hospital. He had had a heart attack in the summer—right in front of the funeral home. "They could have saved themselves the trouble of getting me here," he said with a hearty laugh, "but the ambulance guys got there in time." He had been to the hospital for a follow-up exam. She was chatting about the city—where to get a free cup of coffee, the best soup kitchens in town, and the safest parks. She seemed knowledgeable and had the demeanor of a professional. I assumed from her manner and her vocabulary that she was a social worker or some other kind of counselor, helping him out with useful information.

As I waited for the streetcar, I continued to overhear the exchange between these two people from what seemed like different worlds. I looked fleetingly at the buggy packed with warm clothes and a blanket, a couple of water bottles, and some newspapers. The man and woman chatted nonstop. He was telling her that, though he had lived in Toronto all his adult life, he had never been to the museum or the art gallery or the CN Tower. But, he said with a chuckle, he had visited just about every pub in town.

The woman listened attentively and continued to share information—now, it was about bakeries that gave out free bread at closing time, and which shelters to avoid. She stopped long enough to listen to the man's stories—he was telling her about his childhood in northern Ontario, how he spoke both French and English, and that, years earlier, he had worked in a mine. I wondered about the turns in each of their lives. They looked approximately the same age. But she likely had had a good education—probably a master's degree in social work. He apparently had fallen on hard times at some point in his life.

At last the streetcar arrived. The man and the woman stood up and said their good-byes. But then, to my great surprise, he picked up the backpack and boarded the streetcar. And she grasped the handle of the buggy and, stooped over it, slowly pushed it as she headed toward her next stop, likely the nearby park.

The streetcar continued along its westbound journey. I saw the man strike up a conversation with the fellow beside him. Then I watched as he left by the rear door and walked into an older but still handsome-looking apartment building. As I continued on my way, I thought about how wrong our perceptions and first impressions often are. And I realized that we never know for certain who is really dealing with life's most difficult trials.

The Winning Ticket

Anne Walker

A spontaneous conversation can lift a tremendous weight from a stranger's shoulders.

My sister and I get together every two weeks. We call it "vent night." My dear husband of thirty years is bedridden. A gentle soul, he has always been a great support for everyone. But now his needs are demanding. I also work part-time at home as a bookkeeper. My husband's mind is as sharp as it's always been—he was once a highly respected engineer. But he has a degenerative condition and, as his body continuously weakens, he becomes more and more dependent on me. One of our kids is married, but there's still our university-age daughter at home. My sister, who is married and has two kids in college, looks after our mom. Mom's situation is almost the opposite of my husband's. Physically, she's in reasonable shape for an eighty-year-old woman, but she suffers from Alzheimer's disease. Once capable of multitasking (long before the term was fashionable), as a young widow she managed to support three young kids and raised us to be independent and capable young adults and adults.

"Vent night" is when my sister and I go out for a nice dinner and a glass of wine and catch up on our lives. We give each other progress reports, though unfortunately neither my husband nor my mom is progressing. It's quite the reverse. It breaks our hearts to see the people we love decline. But our evenings together give us something to look forward to and an opportunity to unwind and unload.

A couple of weeks ago, we decided to check out an Italian restaurant. Michelle lives in a suburb south of the city, and I live in a small town to the north. We usually meet at a place we've heard about. We both love good food and have adventurous palates.

The waitress had brought our meals to the table and we were sampling several dishes when a single man walked in and sat at the table next to ours. He was about ten years older than we are—in his early sixties, I would think. The waitress greeted him warmly, and my sister and I assumed he was a regular. Then the waitress looked at us and asked if we were enjoying our meals. "We certainly are," Michelle said enthusiastically. "And thanks so much for your recommendations." The waitress seemed pleased and then asked the man if he was having his usual. Yes, he was, he said. "Minestrone soup—and I'm sure it'll be as good as it was last night."

The man looked in our direction and we exchanged smiles. "So what did the waitress recommend that you like so much?" he asked.

"Oh, we like everything too much," I told him good-naturedly. "But it's all so delicious. I'm having the pasta primavera, and my sister's having scampi."

"It does look delicious," he said. "Enjoy it."

"Oh, no question about that. We always enjoy our food," Michelle volunteered, smiling. "We're sisters and we come from a French family. Food is very important."

"I could understand that," the gentleman said. "French food is wonderful!"

Before long, we were comparing foods—his favorite French dishes; the meals that our mother used to prepare for us (too many to mention); the dishes that his mother used to prepare for him. We learned that he was Jewish, and we told him that Jewish cuisine was near the top of our list. "I love potato pancakes," I said, my mouth starting to water.

His soup arrived, but that didn't stop our conversation. As Michelle and I ate our dinner and he had his soup, the conversation flowed. We told him where we lived and that we liked to meet each other "somewhere in between." He lived in a neighborhood about ten miles from where we were then. I didn't say anything, but thought it surprising that his "regular" place would be so far away from his home.

He told us he was retired and had been an electrician. I said I was a bookkeeper, and Michelle said she used to have a florist shop. We switched topics from food to flowers. Before long, we were comparing our favorite books. At some point, the subject of movies entered the conversation. I must admit nobody was making great progress in their food—we were so busy chatting and comparing notes. Then he introduced himself. "I'm Max," he said.

"Pleased to meet you, Max," I replied. "I'm Anne. And that's Michelle, my sister."

I looked at my watch and saw we had been chatting for an hour and a half. The time had flown.

"Anne," Michelle said, "I think we'd better be going." Then I explained to our new friend that we each had a long drive home.

The waitress brought everyone their bill, and Michelle asked her to pack up the leftovers for her always-hungry sons. Max left some money on the table and told the waitress that he didn't need change. I could see he was a generous tipper.

While Michelle and I waited for the doggy bag, Max got up and told us he'd be back in a moment. He walked out the door and, true to his word, returned in a flash. In his hand was a slip of paper. "I'd like to give you two this lottery ticket," he said as he handed it to us. "I doubt you'll win the jackpot—but I want you to remember how lucky I feel to have met such special people. I can't begin to tell you how much I enjoyed our chat."

A few moments later we parted ways, wishing each other well.

As Michelle and I walked to our cars, we spoke about Max and what an unusually pleasant and upbeat fellow he was. "You know, Anne," Michelle said to me. "We never compared notes on Mom or Doug. This is the first 'vent night' when we didn't vent."

"I didn't even realize that," I commented. "And that's probably why I'm feeling better tonight than I've felt in months. For the first time in ages, I'm feeling grateful—and optimistic."

"That's how I feel, too," Michelle said. "I can't believe what a good mood I'm in."

NEARLY TWO WEEKS went by, and it was time for us to make arrangements for our upcoming "vent night."

"Anne," Michelle said to me. "I know we like to try new places, but I'd love to go back to the Italian restaurant. It would be nice to see our friend Max again."

On "vent night," we parked our cars and met outside the restaurant. It was about the same time we had been there two weeks earlier. We sat at our old table. Max wasn't at "his" table, which was empty, but we figured—or hoped—he'd soon show up. The same waitress was there, but she didn't seem to remember us. We told her that we had liked her recommendations the last time, and would like to try something different.

Our meals arrived—chicken cacciatore and a noodle dish with

seafood. We started to eat, but both of us were preoccupied with the hope that our friend would appear.

About midway through our meal, the waitress came over and asked if we were enjoying her suggestions. "Oh, yes," I said. "But there's something I'd like to ask you."

"Sure," she replied. "What would you like to know?"

"We were here a couple of weeks ago and sat next to a very fine man, about sixty or so," I began. "He told us his name was Max and that he was a regular. We were hoping to see him here again."

"Oh," the waitress said. "I do remember you now. You were chatting with him."

"That's right," Michelle said. "We wanted to continue our conversation."

"I'm sorry to tell you," the waitress said slowly, "but Max hasn't been here since about two days after your visit. We miss him— he came in for a bowl of soup almost every night for nearly a year. He never said much, but he was always sweet. Sometimes he was sad, and one evening he explained that his wife was in the hospital—the one just down the street—and was not getting better. He visited her every day. He would spend most of the day with her—they had no kids and were very devoted to each other. Then, before catching the streetcar home, he'd always stop by for his bowl of soup."

We waited for the waitress to continue.

"Max's wife passed away nearly two weeks ago," she went on.

"It would have been just a couple of days after you met him. He stopped in to tell us that she had died, and to say good-bye because we wouldn't be seeing him anymore. He thanked us for being so nice to him, and he gave us a box of chocolates."

The waitress wiped a tear from the corner of her eye—we could tell that Max had made an impression on her as well.

Michelle and I finished our meals and walked quietly to our cars. We exchanged hardly a word. We were both thinking the same thing, but Michelle spoke first.

"You know, Anne," she said. "We had no idea how sad he must have been that night. His wife must have been terribly ill then. And I'm sure he had no idea of what you and I have been going through, either."

"You're right Michelle," I said. Then, after a pause, I continued. "Isn't it wonderful," I said, "that, for a brief moment, we were able to bring one another out of our sorrows—for each of us to lift a weight from a stranger's shoulders?"

Michelle nodded, and the two of us hugged. We smiled at each other as we began to part ways, and then Michelle stopped and said, "You know, Anne, we never checked the lottery ticket to see if we won something."

"Do we really need to?" I asked quietly.

What I Signed Up to Do

Captain James Lee

When I think of James Lee, I think of two words: *compassion* and *others*. From the first time we met James at the Bible College at Trinity Western University in Langley, British Columbia, I noticed how he bustled about trying to help first-year students settle in and get comfortable in their new dorms. The next time we noticed him was when he helped our daughter around classrooms and halls while she was in her wheelchair. James worked with First Nations people at the Street Service City Mission in Vancouver, where he invited us to speak and entertain at his Christmas banquet for First Nations youth. He has always had an amazing way of working with people of different cultures. He went on to be pastor at the New Beginnings Church in Surrey, British Columbia, and always invited us to his graduations and important stepping-stone parties on his journey. Then he was named chaplain at the Canadian Forces base in Petawawa,

Ontario, doing what he had been trained to do for so many years. Hebrews 12:1 seems to fit him well: ". . . and let us run with endurance the race that is set before us." James loves the race set before him.

I am currently serving as a military chaplain posted to a garrison in Petawawa, Ontario. I joined the Canadian Forces (CF) as a part-time reserve chaplain in August 2011 and transferred to a full-time regular forces chaplain position two years later. Before my full-time service, I had served as an urban missionary among underprivileged children, youth, and families in East Vancouver for about eighteen years.

God laid the desire in my heart to serve as a military chaplain a number of years ago. A part of the history of Korean War (1950–1953) inspired my military services in a significant way. In the summer of 1997, I visited the Korean War Museum at the national cemetery in Seoul to pay my respects to those who had sacrificed their lives for freedom and justice. There, I saw a picture of US Marines frozen to death in the frontline trenches. The winter of 1950 in Korea was exceptionally bitter cold, and nearly a million Chinese troops were mobilized to aid Communist North Korea, which was trying to take over free South Korea through military aggression. Those US Marines, who were there to protect refugees fleeing from the oppressive regime, were not equipped for extreme cold weather and paid the ultimate price. I thought of the wives, children, parents, siblings, and close friends of those marines and the emotional pain they had to face for many years. Some years later, I had a chance to visit the Veterans Memorial in Washington DC. I saw an inscription there, "Freedom is not free," and I went on to read a plaque at the memorial. It was inscribed, "Our nation honors her sons and daughters who answered the call to defend a country they never knew and a people they never met."

What I saw was a priceless picture of sacrifice, honor, and courage painted by the men and women in uniform. I shed tears that day. That picture and those words have echoed in my heart ever since, especially in times of hardship, leading me to serve the nation and God years later.

In the summer of 2013, I answered the call to serve full-time with the Canadian Forces and was posted to Petawawa, a military-friendly town about an hour and a half's drive northwest of Ottawa. On the first day of duty, I was assigned to a Field Hospital Medical Unit and met with its commanding officer (CO) and regiment sergeant major (RSM). Thankfully, the CO valued the chaplain's role and was highly supportive of my work within the unit. One of the chaplain's roles is to work closely with the CO and RSM as part of the command team and to advise the chain of command on matters of ethics and unit morale. This unit has about 350 troops who are medics, doctors, nurses, dentists, health-care administrators, specialists, and other military medical professionals. I provide chaplain care to all members and their families. It is a busy job, but enjoyable.

One of the things I am doing with my unit members is morning physical training. I care about each member, and the troops seem to be appreciative of me as their padre. I love the troops, and I know they are deeply loved by God.

In October, I participated in my unit's field training for three weeks. This exercise was to enhance the readiness of the troops deployed for humanitarian operations. We were preparing for situations where the forces would be rapidly deployed internationally, with forty-eight-hours' notice, to a vulnerable region and population. This would be a highly intensive and demanding operation because the troops have to move massive field hospital structures and equipment to the designated region within a limited time frame. At the time, I was sleeping, eating, and hanging out with the troops in the Ontario bush. I had Thanksgiving dinner with them and, on Sundays, I facilitated and led field worship services for those who had a Christian faith background.

A real disaster occurred in early November as Typhoon Haiyan devastated the central region of the Philippines. The Canadian Forces were called on to respond to this crisis. They were commanded to execute medical relief work in the typhoon-ravaged city of Iloilo, the home base of Canadian medical teams and engineers in the Philippines. I was involved in the process of prescreening selected CF members who were placed on standby for deployment there. From my medical services units, about fifty members were part of the Disaster Assistance Response Team. Another fifty members from my units were on standby as of November 15.

To be deployed with forty-eight-hours' notice, the troops were required to jump over countless hurdles and go through an intense assessment process. Here are some of the things they had to do in those few hours: obtain up to seven vaccination shots, secure valid passports, have their medical and dental conditions screened, update their physical-fitness reports, and undergo interviews by a chaplain. As well, the troops' personal and family lives needed to be entirely rearranged within several hours. In one case, a member had to organize care for his two small children. Christmas plans were put on hold in case the troops would remain in the Philippines past December 25. The troops had to cancel all other appointments and pack up all their personal items and military kit. They were lucky if they got a few hours' sleep during those two days.

One of the nurses who had participated in a field exercise with me a month earlier received a call from her supervisor on the morning of November 11, Remembrance Day. She was instructed to report to Canadian Forces Base Petawawa, a four-hour drive from her home, within several hours. That meant she had to drop everything, pack her personal items and essentials, and hit the road in just two hours. She was very tired by the time she saw me. She also had to complete the readiness checklist, go through the assessment process, and pack up her personal and military kits before boarding the aircraft headed to the Philippines. She is a conscientious young woman with a kind heart, who attends a Baptist church in Montreal. I could see that she would give the best care possible to injured or needy locals. It is physically and mentally exhausting work, especially in a different time zone with tropical temperatures. But I knew she would do much more than what her duty called her to do. I had conducted screening interviews with about fifty CF members on standby. They were all highly motivated for altruistic reasons. When I asked why he wanted to be deployed, one young medical technician replied, "Sir, this is what I signed up to do—help others."

I remained in Petawawa and assisted the troops in a rear-party support role—supporting their families as needed. I regularly received updates on the Philippines mission. With the death toll from the super typhoon Haiyan (called "Yolanda" by the population) inching closer to 6,000, the Filipino people had little to be cheerful about. As of December 13, government disaster management officials placed the number of deaths at 5,959, while the injured and missing remained at 27,022 and 1,779, respectively. One medical officer stated,

We have Mobile Medical Teams (MMTs) out every day. An MMT consists of a medical doctor, physician assistant, and two medical technicians. They average about 110 patients each day per team. The public is so happy to see us. People stop us on the street to shake our hands and say thank you. The work is exhausting in the heat, and many of the communities we are serving are remote and are two or three hours' transport ride away. The devastation is all around: tons of debris, broken homes, and buildings. It will take years to clean everything.

A task-force surgeon reported that the most common ailments were open wounds, abrasions, or gashes as a result of storm damage. Many people had been cut with metal, nails, or bamboo, the primary building products used on the islands. Others had contracted infections due to lack of clean water and sanitation or suffered from respiratory problems. Those with serious or life-threatening injuries had, fortunately, made it to a hospital, he added.

These men and women in uniform have made a difference for many people in the Philippines, and we have reason to be proud of our troops. They have demonstrated their dedication to help those they did not know. These stories of sacrifice, duty, honor, courage, and compassion continue to unfold. I am grateful for opportunities to be part of these stories, serving among troops who desire to make a difference for the better.

Good News Stories

Our newspapers are filled with sad and upsetting stories—sometimes we even hesitate to look at the headlines. But occasionally an article conveys something remarkable about the human spirit or reveals an act of extreme kindness and decency. Here are some "good news stories" that were recently in the news.

"SOMETIMES PEOPLE HAVE IT WORSE"

On a cold November night, New York City police officer Larry DePrimo saw a barefoot, homeless man in Times Square. The policeman went into a nearby store and, with his own money, bought a pair of one-hundred-dollar all-weather boots and presented them to the man. The incident would have gone unnoticed—an anonymous act of kindness by a policeman on his beat—but a tourist from Arizona witnessed the selfless act and snapped a photo with her cell phone. She then emailed it to the

New York Police Department, and, before long, the photo was an Internet sensation and the twenty-five-year-old officer a hero.

Officer DePrimo said that his own feet were freezing that night—he was wearing two pairs of socks—and added that the man's face "lit up" at the sight of the boots. The two men never exchanged names, and the policeman still keeps the receipt for the boots in his vest. It reminds him that "sometimes people have it worse." (From *People* magazine, November 29, 2012)

WHAT YOU'VE NEVER HAD, YOU NEVER MISS

Violet and Allen Large, a retired couple from rural Nova Scotia, bought a lottery ticket on July 14, 2010. When Violet read the winning numbers in the local newspaper the next morning, she couldn't believe her eyes. The couple had just won $11.2 million.

The Larges, who lived modestly, decided they had everything they wanted. So when they hit the jackpot, they began making a list of charities and community groups that could use the money. "That money . . . was nothing," the seventy-five-year-old Allen Large said. "We have each other." By the time they had finished, the list was two pages.

The couple donated 98 percent of their winnings to hospitals, their local fire departments, churches, cemeteries, the Red Cross, Salvation Army, and several organizations that fight cancer, Alzheimer's disease, and diabetes. At the time they won, Violet was recovering from surgery and chemotherapy treatments for cancer. She said hand-delivering the money to various groups kept her spirits up.

In the summer of 2011, Violet Large died at the Colchester Regional Hospital in Truro, Nova Scotia. The hospital foundation, which was one of the charities the Larges supported, issued the following statement: "She gave us many lasting gifts: the reminder of how precious life is, how to mean what you say and say what you mean, to be a good person and a good neighbor, to always do what you say you will and, perhaps the most important for a happy life, to want what you have; not have what you want." (From the *Toronto Star*, November 11, 2010; and CBC News, July 18, 2011)

"ANY CITIZEN WOULD DO IT— IT'S NOTHING SPECIAL"

JOHN MALKOVICH is a Hollywood actor famous for his roles in movies, on the stage, and on television. But on June 6, 2013, he was just an "ordinary bystander" in Toronto whose path crossed with a visitor in danger. In a freak accident, Jim Walpole of Ohio tripped on the sidewalk, stumbled, and got caught on hotel scaffolding, tearing open his neck. As he lay bleeding in the street, a man ran over and administered the emergency first aid that may have saved Mr. Walpole's life. As the stranger pressed on Mr. Walpole's neck, he explained he was trying to stop the bleeding and comforted him by saying, "My name is John, and you are going to be all right."

"He really knew what he was doing; that's why I thought he was a doctor," the visitor's wife, a nurse, later said. "He had no qualms about getting blood all over him; that would be a real concern for some people." Only later would the couple learn that the bystander was an Academy Award–nominated actor. ("I don't see that many movies," said Ms. Walpole.) When interviewed, Mr. Malkovich said simply, "Any citizen would do it—it's nothing special." (From the *National Post*, June 9, 2013)

A MUTT NAMED PEBBLE

DR. ELISE HÉON, the chief ophthalmologist at Toronto's Hospital for Sick Children, was in Arizona for a relaxing spa vacation. It was Thursday morning, and she had just flown in. "I was getting ready to go have breakfast," she later explained, "and the weather was perfect. So I said I'd go for a little hike before breakfast."

Little did Dr. Héon realize that she would spend more than twenty-four hours stranded on a narrow ledge, suspended seven hundred feet above the floor of a remote canyon after she lost track of a trail covered in pine needles.

Dr. Héon was reported missing that night, and rescue teams

started their search. The next morning, "determined to be heard," she cried out for help. Sally Gebler heard one of her screams, but doubted what it was until Pebble, her three-year-old mutt, started barking. "I know Pebble's behaviors," Ms. Gebler said, "and I know when I really need to pay attention."

Ms. Gebler's husband quickly grabbed his GPS, hiked in closer to Dr. Héon, and passed on the coordinates to two sheriff's deputies. Eventually, a team of paramedic rock climbers reached Dr. Héon and persuaded her to climb up fifty feet so she could be rescued by helicopter.

Today, the doctor credits her survival to the keen ears of a mutt named Pebble. (From the *Globe and Mail* and CTV News, April 6, 2013)

A RANDOM "FRIEND" SAVES A MAN'S LIFE

TWO WOMEN FROM OPPOSITE ENDS of the world were playing the online game Words with Friends. During the game, Georgie Fletcher of Queensland, Australia, told Beth Legler, of Blue Springs, Missouri, that her husband, Simon, was feeling under the weather. Beth asked Georgie to describe the symptoms, since her own husband, Larry, was a doctor. Hearing the symptoms, Dr. Legler provided the following advice: get Simon to a doctor immediately. As it turned out, Simon had a 99 percent blockage in an artery near his heart. Had he not gone to the hospital that day, he surely would have died. (From CBS News, January 16, 2012; and *Reader's Digest* magazine, December 2012)

A RUNAWAY CAR AND A MIRACLE IN NEW MEXICO

As Lezlie Bicknell of Albuquerque, New Mexico, pulled into a gas station parking lot, she saw two unattended toddlers in a locked minivan parked beside her. One of the children was sitting in the driver's seat, and Lezlie saw the child shift the van into gear. As the van begin to drift backward, Lezlie instinctively jumped out of her own truck to help.

Meanwhile, Lezlie's own vehicle began rolling backward. "I must've knocked my own car in gear jumping out," she later explained. "I left the door wide open." Lezlie's truck managed to pull out ahead of the minivan and ended up behind it—miraculously preventing the van from rolling into the traffic along a busy road. (From the *Daily Mail*, July 11, 2012; and *Reader's Digest* magazine, December 2012)

PART FOUR
Goodness and Gentleness

And the Lord passed before him [Moses] and proclaimed, "The Lord, the Lord God, merciful and gracious, longsuffering, and abounding in goodness and truth."
—Exodus 34:6

Preserve me, O God, for in You I put my trust.
O my soul, you have said to the Lord,
"You are my Lord,
My goodness is nothing apart from You."
—Psalm 16:1–2

I would have lost heart, unless I had believed
That I would see the goodness of the Lord
In the land of the living.
—Psalm 27:13

Therefore consider the goodness and severity of God: on those who fell, severity; but toward you, goodness, if you continue in His goodness.
—Romans 11:22

But the fruit of the Spirit is love, joy, peace, longsuffering, kindness, goodness, faithfulness, gentleness, self-control. Against such there is no law.
—Galatians 5:22–23

Do not let your adornment be merely outward—arranging the hair, wearing gold, or putting on fine apparel—
rather let it be the hidden person of the heart, with the incorrupt ible beauty of a gentle and quiet spirit, which is very precious in the sight of God.
—1 Peter 3:3–4

Let your gentleness be known to all men. The Lord is at hand.
—Philippians 4:5

WHEN WE GIVE CHEERFULLY

If we have no peace, it is because we have forgotten that we belong to each other.

—Mother Teresa

The ideals which have always shone before me and filled me with joy are goodness, beauty, and truth.

—Albert Einstein

When we give cheerfully and accept gratefully, everyone is blessed.

—Maya Angelou

Every time you smile at someone, it is an action of love, a gift to that person, a beautiful thing.

—Mother Teresa

Wrinkles should merely indicate where smiles have been.

—Mark Twain

Tillie, my beloved missionary who passed away in October 2013, was encouraging us to pray for our loved ones. She shared this prayer that she once heard a little girl say: "God, bless Mommy and Daddy, my brothers and sisters. And God, do look after Yourself— because if anything goes wrong with You, we are in deep trouble!"

—Recalled by Margaret Fishback Powers

The best thing to give to your enemy is forgiveness; to an opponent, tolerance; to a friend, your heart; to your child, a good example; to a father, deference; to your mother, conduct that will make her proud of you; to yourself, respect; to all men, charity.

—Arthur James Balfour

Good words are worth much, and cost little.

—George Herbert

If you must speak ill of another, do not speak it, write it in the sand near the water's edge.

—Napoleon Hill

If there is righteousness in the heart, there will be beauty in character; if there is beauty in character, there will be harmony in the home. If there is harmony in the home, there will be order in the nation; if there is order in the nation, there will be peace in the world.

—Chinese proverb

God sees hearts as we see faces.

—George Herbert

The most valuable gift you can give another is a good example.

—Unknown

Bedside Manner

Suzanne Goodman

A person's caring nature reveals itself in unexpected ways and at important times.

Around the time she turned eighty, my mom was diagnosed with Parkinson's disease. At first, the tremors weren't too troublesome, and she wouldn't let anything slow her down. She continued volunteering at the local hospital in our small town. She worked on the floors—visiting and providing reassurance to patients. She never let on that she had been a nurse. She was there as a volunteer, and her "job," as she called it, was to provide comfort to people.

Around the time Mom turned eighty-five, Parkinson's was beginning to take a toll. Around that time, she felt she could no longer do a proper "job" at the hospital, so she retired.

At first, my mom saw a general neurologist. He put her through the usual tests and regularly checked the effectiveness of her medications. But after a year, Dr. G. determined that Mom should see a specialist in movement disorders. He arranged for Mom to see a highly regarded physician who had recently moved to Toronto, about an hour's drive for us.

I had heard about a service that provided information about doctors, and I phoned to see what they had to say about Dr. M. "Excellent diagnostician," I was told. "But she isn't warm and is short on bedside manner." I balanced the first comment against the second, and decided the first quality outweighed the second.

We had an appointment, and on the first visit, Dr. M. asked the usual questions and ran a battery of tests. She wasn't what you would describe as "warm," but she wasn't "cold," either. She did what many people do when they talk with older people—spoke extra loudly, assuming my mom was hard of hearing. But the doctor got an A for effort and was generous with her time. She also changed my mom's prescription and was careful in checking her history and other medications.

The new medication seemed to help—at least, the Parkinson's didn't progress as quickly as it had over the past year or two. But Mom was growing frailer (the tremors burn calories)—despite milk shakes and larger helpings of her favorite ice cream.

Twice yearly we saw Dr. M. She still tended to talk louder than she needed to, but managed to smile and even seemed pleased when Mom told her that her kids, whose photos were displayed on the desk, were "sweet."

Mom turned ninety and, despite increased dosages of medication, the Parkinson's had reached a critical point. As well, it was a particularly difficult year. For the first time, my strong-willed mother seemed to have given up. Friends had passed away—that's what happens when you reach ninety, but knowing that doesn't make it any easier. Mom felt she was a "burden," though I reminded her of what one of her doctors had once explained to her: "When your daughter was young and carried a 'package,' you were the one who held the door open for her. Now you're holding the 'package,' and she's opening the door."

It was hard to see Mom sad and losing her self-confidence. I tried reminding Mom of "Footprints in the Sand," one of her favorite poems, and told her that, even though this was among the "most troublesome times" of her life, she was being watched over. She wondered who was "watching." I told her she would soon know.

It was time for the twice-yearly appointment with Dr. M. We had a long drive to the downtown hospital. What started as a sunny December day turned threatening, and it appeared a blizzard was looming. Mom was subdued during the drive; my mind was on the weather and what the driving conditions would be like on our way home. There was generally a long wait in the doctor's office, and I had thoughts of heading home in a blizzard during rush hour. Usually on these drives, I needed to comfort Mom. It wouldn't be an easy drive for either of us.

I parked the car and we slowly headed to the entrance of the medical building. We got out of the elevator and walked into the predictably crowded waiting room. It was a humbling sight: people of all ages—some young and relatively healthy looking, most accompanied by a child or parent or spouse—were waiting to see this world-renowned doctor. I glanced outside the large window. The days were short and it was already late afternoon. Looking at the number of people in the waiting room and guessing how long each one would spend with the doctor, I knew we'd be here for a couple of hours.

I helped my mom to a seat and then checked in with the receptionist. She looked at the health card and verified the address, then reached for a file folder and placed it at the bottom of a small mountain of folders. Each folder told a story of someone's declining condition—a multitude of tests, reports, assessments. I returned to the waiting area and sat beside Mom. I continued to glance out the window, knowing the roads would only get worse.

My eyes then darted toward the hallway. A patient was leaving the doctor's office. We were one file folder closer to the top. A few minutes later, Dr. M. approached the reception area. She looked at the files, she scanned the faces in the waiting room, and then she looked at the large window and through it the storm brewing outside. "Mrs C.," Dr. M. said, glancing at us. "You're next. Please come with me."

That was my mom, and I knew there was a mistake. So did the receptionist. "Oh, no, Dr. M., she isn't next," she whispered to the doctor.

"Oh yes she is," the doctor replied.

I don't like to "jump a line," but I realized that the doctor had assessed everyone in the room, taken note of the storm, and realized that we probably had the longest drive ahead and that Mom was probably the frailest person in the waiting room.

We followed Dr. M. down the long hallway to her office.

Then she held the door open for both of us.

A Tribute to Alice

Paula Margaret Callahan

Some beautiful friendships begin in unexpected ways.

I often have people come up to me and say, "Oh, I know you through the first chapter of your mother's book *Footprints: The True Story That Inspired Millions*. How are you now?" They of course recall the story of how I fell over a waterfall and into a deep glacier pool and miraculously survived. I always reply, "I'm fine, thank you,"—mostly because I have become a rather private person, and also because I don't want to take my time to share details. I do know that some people truly care—and not only care, but love me enough to be able to handle and assimilate the truth. I need these truth-seekers in my life to probe beyond my casual "fine, thank you" and discover for themselves who God is continually remaking me to become. One of these people I allow to probe beneath the surface is Alice (Lucie) Kinnear, whom I have affectionately known as "Miss Lucie" for the past twenty-five years.

My recovery from my fall was much slower than we had initially prayed for it to be. Honestly, most days I was simply grateful to be alive, yet in such pain that I was overwhelmed and prayed the Lord would see fit to call me home to Him. About a year into my recovery, when I had grown somewhat accustomed to the chronic pain and medications prescribed, a family friend suggested that a friend of hers just "might" be able to help me. I was more than willing to try, and my determined (and desperate) mother was thrilled to drive me to get some possible help. (The neurological and nerve damage to my brain and right side rendered me unable to drive for about three years post-accident. Even after that time, I was extremely cautious since I blacked out if I stood up too quickly. And to this day, I have no feeling in the fingers of my right hand.)

Miss Lucie was an elegantly coiffed and spectacularly dressed older lady who did reflexology out of her just-as-lovely apartment. As a believer who had traveled extensively and seen many types of healing practices, I was hesitant to get into anything that even remotely suggested "voodoo." But, faced with some humbling, disabling, excruciating pain, I was willing to hear what this Christian retired doctor's assistant had to say.

After explaining the history of reflexology and how God created our bodies in such an interdependent yet regenerative manner, Miss Lucie gave me my first "foot rub." "Foot rub" is a rather innocuous term. I was shocked when I woke up after a couple of hours and spotted my patient mother sipping tea with this gentle woman. I had been taking sleeping pills for months to help offset the painkillers—in a vicious cycle to find relief. And here, Miss Lucie and my mum had had a delightful English teatime while I snored, completely comfortable in the special chair of Miss Lucie. After Miss Lucie assured me I hadn't drooled in front of her, I promised I would return again as soon as Mum could manage to bring me.

Thus began a beautiful friendship that has endured over all these years.

Miss Lucie basically pulled me onto my feet—through my feet. She always encouraged my sunny, funny disposition, and I credit her with saving my life both literally and figuratively. She monitored me even after I moved to the United States and married an American—and even came to visit me in Idaho after my son was born in 2000.

Just being pregnant was a shock, since I was not supposed to bear children because the accident had damaged my "baby-making" organs. Calvin arrived more than five weeks early, and Miss Lucie came to stay and encourage me in my wonderful blessing. One morning she said, "My dear, I think you need to go directly to the hospital. You don't look well to me, and I'll watch the baby while you go." I didn't know what to think. After all, I was used to feeling sick *all* the time and, as a new mother, I thought I was just slow in recovering. But I respected Miss Lucie enough to drive to the local hospital, where I promptly fainted in the lobby with a 105-degree fever. Apparently, mastitis was covered in one of the child-birthing classes I had missed. (The baby arrived way too early! I guess I graduated, however, since he was actually born.) God was certainly gracious to bring Miss Lucie to our sleep-deprived home, and she has always had a special affinity for my "preemie" boy.

Last summer, my now thirteen-year-old son (whose little hand at birth was the size of his papa's thumbnail but who is now taller than him) and I went to Victoria, British Columbia, to visit Miss Lucie. She is now ninety-eight years old, and we want every trip to count. Miss Lucie is mellowing graciously and encouraging her patients to put their best foot forward and get on with life.

And I am still blessed by her continual example of kindness, good humor, friendliness, and godliness. As we were leaving to catch the ferry from Victoria, she received a reflexology newsletter that mentioned her. It was such a wonderful surprise and pleasure to add my sincere compliments and ask for a copy to share with others. No tribute could ever be enough to pay this most important and special woman . . . a gift to my life. Congratulations, Miss Lucie, on a life of dedication and giving to others. You are our heroine.

A TRIBUTE TO ALICE KINNEAR

Ryan Gunther, Reflexology Association of British Columbia
Alice Kinnear was born in Ontario in 1915. She moved
to Vancouver at the age of nine, where she lived through
the Great Depression of the 1930s. Shortly after the
Second World War, Alice began work as a receptionist
in a medical doctor's office. There, through a conversation with a visiting patient, the interest in reflexology
was stimulated. Over the following years, Alice pursued
her interest, learning and mastering the technique and,
through practice, establishing a clientele.

Alice successfully completed a course in the Ingham
Reflexology Method in July 1974, receiving a certificate
signed by Eunice Ingham herself. In 1978 she successfully
completed a written and practical examination, becoming registered with the National Institute of Reflexology.
In 1995 she received a certificate of recognition from
the International Council of Reflexologists. Throughout
her years of practicing reflexology, she also participated
in many activities to promote reflexology. In 1996 Alice
became an honorary member of the Reflexology Association of British Columbia.

One of her most treasured reflexology success stories
was the treatment of a gentleman with polio. In a des-

perate act, the man's wife called Alice and explained to her that one of his legs had turned black and the doctors wanted to amputate. Alice immediately began a regimen of foot reflexology treatments, and within four months, the discoloration retreated and the leg became what she describes as "pink as a baby's skin."

Alice lives in Victoria and, at the age of ninety-eight, practices reflexology on a handful of select clients. We congratulate Alice on her many accomplishments and thank her for her dedication and contributions to the health and well-being of her clients, as well as to the advancement of reflexology and the Reflexology Association of British Columbia.

What the Wind Blew In

Joseph Liebman

Do not go where the path may lead, go instead where there is no path and leave a trail.

—Ralph Waldo Emerson

Somewhere in one of his essays, Ralph Waldo Emerson writes that if you look deeply enough, you will see that everything is connected. He says it's like the wind. The wind brings all sorts of things from lots of places, but it always seems to be heading toward one destination: your hat.

Chalk it up to the wind, but our little branch library in San Francisco has been packed these past few days. Even the old-timers can't recall such a windy September. "Must be Katrina," said one, even though the hurricane happened last month and was more than two thousand miles away. Despite the spike in attendance, reference questions are as scarce as ever. Most of the young-timers can't recall when they last asked one. Why should they, when they have Google? (How do you think I knew that New Orleans was two thousand miles away?) Questions are what I like most about my job. Questions are to librarians what computers are to kids. Here, let me ask the one who's sitting just to my right.

"Excuse me, have you asked your librarian any questions lately?"

"No, I don't think so . . . Wait a minute. Yesterday I asked her one."

"Do you remember what it was?"

"Sure. I asked her can I have another hour on the computer."

Well, not exactly the kind of question I had in mind. But still, people, especially kid people, think of the librarian as the person with all the answers. I keep a file called "Reference Question of the Month." July: "What do you call a male ladybug?" (The answer, less engaging than the question, is a beetle.)

Last month, there was one question that I would get over and over, and the answer was always the same: "Not yet." The question came from Kathryn at the Chief of Branches Office: "Is your fax machine working?" Our fax machine hadn't been working for weeks. And for weeks, Kathryn had been trying to get the engineers to come down to our far-flung branch. (If you look at a map of San Francisco, Ocean View is barely on it.) Last week, the boys dropped by. And while they managed to get it to work, it still wheezes and coughs and gives pitiful sighs.

It was the last Thursday in September, and a small family group was standing outside the library, waiting to get in. There are still some folks in the neighborhood who don't know that we open at one on Thursdays, but these didn't look like neighborhood folks. They were (I assumed) a husband and wife and a small child held in its father's arms. Fortunately, it was just a few minutes before one, so I went over to the door and pointed to the sign outside and the clock on the wall. It was then that I noticed why the father was holding the baby. The mother was grasping onto a cane. I let them in.

As soon as they were inside, they collapsed onto the nearest chairs, a look of infinite weariness crossing their faces. They had just come from Mississippi, having lost everything in the hurricane. Thanks to a minister in Gulfport, they had found shelter with a family on Randolph Street, just down the block from our library. If you want to get federal assistance, they had been informed, you must register at the Federal Emergency Management Agency's website and FEMA will contact you by email. The trouble was that they didn't have an address, email or otherwise. So they had come to the library. The other trouble was that they had never used a computer. So click by click, we guided them through the websites and set up a Yahoo email account. Some of the weariness ebbed from their faces. And all the while, the baby, smiling, happily turned the pages of an oversized copy of *Where's Waldo.*

But because troubles come in threes, there was another technical problem. "The email they sent me says I have to fax them a copy of my social security card," said the husband. "Do you all have a fax machine I can use?"

Now the closest fax machine is at Kinko's about three miles from the library, and the family had no car. Actually, the closest fax machine is the one in the library, but it's restricted to use by the library staff. So I bent the rule, explaining that we could make this a one-time exception, adding that since it was for staff use only, I would send the fax. With a wheeze and a heave, off went the fax. An hour went by, and then a fax came back, saying that the information had been received, and that a carpentry job had been found in San Francisco. The man was to report for work the following morning. This time, it wasn't only the baby who was smiling.

Later that day, a reader took out a book called *The Roots of Coincidence*. And I thought about a family from Mississippi being washed up on the shores of Ocean View Library. I also thought about a hurricane named Katrina and an angel at the Chief of Branches named Kathryn who insisted on getting our fax machine working. And I thought about *Where's Waldo* and Ralph Waldo Emerson. And I thought about the baby's smile, and I felt connected.

Chopsticks and Forks

Jane Sato

Look beyond superficial differences and learn something about others . . . and about ourselves.

"Why is he looking at us?" I asked myself. I was sitting in a Japanese restaurant, chatting with a friend, and noticed the older man at the table next to ours glancing in our direction. Immediately his attention returned to his tempura, but I wondered why he was so interested in my conversation.

I was in Toronto for a conference. I had flown in from Calgary and arranged to meet an old girlfriend for lunch. She recommended this place, saying "there are always lots of Japanese customers here, so the food has to be good." Although I had lived in Canada for over a decade now, I was born in Tokyo and grew up in Japan—so my friend was cautious about her choice of restaurant. I attended university in Toronto but hadn't been back to the city for many years. Shortly after graduation, I got a job in Alberta. During my years in the country, I've become thoroughly Canadian—a western Canadian.

We were now talking animatedly, comparing notes about her family and my job and reminiscing about our days at school. Then I told her that my mother would be flying in from Tokyo later today. I had planned for my mom and me to take a driving vacation back to Calgary, stopping in small towns along the way, and now I was wondering if the trip was such a good idea. I explained to my friend that after lunch, I'd be heading to the airport to meet my mother. My friend told me that I could take the subway to the Kipling station and then catch a bus to the airport. That's when I noticed the man looking our way. Perhaps he was seeing what we had ordered. I'm used to that when I go to a Japanese restaurant. People assume I'm ordering something "authentic," and they're curious to see what it is.

After the man went back to his meal, I noticed how awkward he was with his chopsticks. He couldn't quite get the hang of them, but persevered nevertheless. "Eating with chopsticks is the easiest thing in the world," I said to my friend in amusement. "How could anyone be so clumsy? Why wouldn't he just ask for a fork?"

My friend and I continued chatting, she about our days at school and me about the driving trip I had planned for my mother and me.

"Maybe it wasn't such a brilliant idea," I said anxiously. "The scenery will be beautiful, but I haven't spent so much time with my mom in over ten years. And just the two of us in a car! I'm a modern Canadian now, and my mother is old-fashioned and traditional. I'm not sure if my mom and I have much in common anymore. And now I'm wondering what she'll think of the every-day Canadians we'll meet at towns along our journey. It may turn out to be a clash of cultures, I'm afraid."

My friend reassured me that everything would go well. "Canadians are friendly," she reminded me. "Your mother will have a great time." But I wasn't convinced. And the more it weighed on my mind, the more I worried about the trip. What would we talk about after the first day—or even after the first few hours?

Soon the conversation took another direction as my friend showed me pictures of her husband, her kids, and her sprawling house in the suburbs. My mind, however, was somewhere else. I was thinking about the upcoming road trip, about how I had changed since leaving Japan. Would my mom be proud of my professional accomplishments? Or would she be disappointed that I hadn't married and had a family—hadn't taken the same path that my friend had followed? And as my friend rambled on about her husband's job, her kids' camp, and the big new swimming pool, I was caught up in my own thoughts. Maybe my anxiety wasn't just about the relationship between my mother and me and the differences that had evolved between us. Maybe I was unsure about the road I had chosen to take.

As my thoughts and emotions played havoc in my mind, I glanced at the man at the table nearby. He had finished his meal and was paying his bill. As he put his change away, he reached into his wallet. Then, instead of heading to the door, he walked over to my table. Why was he doing that? My friend was busy talking about her kids' soccer games, and the gentleman stood there, waiting for her to pause. When she did—finally—he spoke to me. "I'm sorry to interrupt you," he said hesitantly, "and I apologize for eavesdropping earlier in your conversation." I looked at him confused and a little annoyed, wondering what he was going to say next. Then he continued. "I overheard that your mother will be visiting," he went on haltingly. "I'm assuming she's a senior, like me. So here are a couple of seniors' subway tickets for her to use."

And with that, he turned away and left.

"How odd!" my friend said, looking bewildered.

I sat there in complete silence—and suddenly the chaos stirring inside my mind calmed down. In that magic moment, through one simple gesture, I knew things would be all right. A stranger—a person I had criticized for something as superficial as using chopsticks in a clumsy way—had shown me that people are thoughtful and kind. That's all that counted. Did it matter whether you had a smart apartment in the city or a sprawling home in the country, a job you could be proud of or a family to look after? Who cared if you used chopsticks or a fork?

Suddenly a tremendous weight lifted from my shoulders. I was ready to head to the airport, greet my mom with a big hug from her loving daughter, and show her the senior tickets that a stranger had provided as her welcome to a beautiful new country.

A Lifeline from My Son-in-Law

Judith Landy

If you want something done, they say, ask a busy person. Sometimes, you don't even have to ask.

My life hit rock bottom nearly twenty years ago. At the age of sixty, I went through a serious depression that no therapist, no medication, no well-meaning friend or uplifting phrase seemed able to alleviate. Severe anxiety attacks and poor sleep turned me into a hopeless mess. Until that time, I had been an independent, positive-thinking woman. Widowed for ten years and retired for about that long, I was involved in rewarding volunteer work, subscribed to the theater, and enjoyed my own company. My three children—all out of town—were healthy and well-established, although one of my daughters was just coming out of a difficult divorce. My grandchildren and I had a close relationship.

If I have to pinpoint an event that led me into this abyss, it would be the forced move from my spacious and affordable apartment in downtown Vancouver, with its beautiful ocean view. My landlord had found a "relative" to live in my apartment—a loophole, I assume, that forced me out and allowed him to increase the rent of my cozy home. I found another apartment in my neighborhood—smaller, darker, and more expensive. And every time I walked by the old building, I was filled with a sense of loss and grief that only deepened.

I tried to hide my misery when I spoke to my children, but they were smart enough to know that something was wrong. I assured them I was fine, just a little down because of the apartment situation. The kids suggested I visit, but I found some excuse or other. They had busy lives, and I didn't want to intrude.

I could have dealt with the change in my apartment, but I think its loss brought back a host of memories of past losses and triggered emotions that made me think negatively. My friends noticed the change in my mood, and Betty, one of the dearest people I've ever known, decided to phone my daughter Sue in New Brunswick. Sue wasn't home, but it seems Betty had a long conversation with my son-in-law, Gord.

They say that if you want something done, ask a busy person. With Gord—a lawyer with a busy practice—nobody even has to ask. He sizes up a situation and then takes action. He caught a plane that weekend, assessed the situation, and soon began a campaign to convince me to move to Fredericton, to be closer to my daughter and her family.

Before long, Gord and Sue convinced me to make the move. Some of my friends thought I was foolish, but others thought it would be good for me to be with my family.

My daughter soon helped me find an excellent therapist, and within a year, I felt I was beginning a happy new chapter in life. I enrolled in a course at the university, found a sunny apartment, and gradually began making new friends. Now eighty, I continue to enjoy my life in Fredericton.

Although proudly independent, I know I am lucky to have my daughter and son-in-law close by. And over the years, I have seen my son-in-law reach out to others—my grandchildren, his own friends in need, clients, and even complete strangers—the way he reached out to me.

Give Your Flowers to the Living

Sally Sue Lucas

"Make someone happy," are the lyrics of an old song. "And you will be happy too."

My mom had a favorite expression: "Give your flowers to the living. If you love them, tell them so." She not only spoke those words, but lived them too. Mom was always delighted to pay a compliment or let someone know they were special.

I can think of many examples. In the years before Google searches, Mom tracked down her high school Latin teacher and told her how much she had been affected by her kindness and encouragement. At her church, she befriended a family of new immigrants and encouraged the young daughter to pursue her dream of being a concert pianist. After seeing a play, she would wait at the stage door to tell an actor how meaningful his performance had been to her.

In her last years, when she was mostly housebound, she continued to brighten the lives of others. Her doctors loved her. Mom would admire their children's drawings that adorned office walls.

After Mom passed away, it was heartwarming to read some letters and cards she had saved. Among the notes I found was this one from a neighbor:

Dear Mrs. L.,

I do hope you don't mind my occasionally sending you flowers, which I will not be around to enjoy. Today we're headed to the cottage, and this little centerpiece and plant will languish unappreciated if they're left in our apartment. They remind me of you—colorful, pretty, and nice to be near. I hope you'll enjoy them.

Hilda

It seems that people had given flowers to her, just as she had given them to others.

Let's Hear It for Our Aunts!

Frances Jenkins

Only an Aunt . . . can give hugs like a mother, can keep secrets like a sister, and share love like a friend.

—Author unknown

I often think about my aunts. After Sunday school, I'd frequently drop in to see Aunt Sylvia, who lived near our church. I could talk about anything with Aunt Sylvia. She never judged me, she talked to me as an equal—not as an eight-year-old—and her counsel was always wise. Decades later, I think about her almost every day. She was my confidante.

And then there was my beloved Aunt Ann. When my marriage was falling apart, I knew I could always count on her kindnesses to melt away my anxiety. "Put your feet up, honey," she would say, "and I'll make us a pot of tea." She'd sing some of my favorite childhood songs and provide emotional support through some of the lowest points in my life.

Aunt Lois, my glamorous aunt, never married. She held a high position at a bank and lived in a swanky apartment with a Siamese cat named Venus. When I visited her, I felt like a movie star. Aunt Lois was my "cool" aunt. We'd go out for dinner (she let me pick the place). She was also generous and helped pay for my education. Aunt Lois encouraged me to follow my dreams.

Recently, I was thinking about the roles that our aunts play. They are loving and nurturing, and often less judgmental and more fun than moms. Aunts—and their nieces and nephews— have the best of both worlds. I've read that the relationship between a niece and her aunt is often more reciprocal than the one between a daughter and her mom, probably because there are fewer responsibilities.

Although I'm still waiting to become an aunt, I was reminded of the special bond when I recently chatted with two friends, Joyce and Barbara.

Over dinner, Joyce talked about her nephew, Marc. Marc has an autism spectrum disorder. He has problems interacting in social situations, and his behavior is repetitive. At family functions, Marc will dominate the conversation until his mother or father gently reminds him to let other people talk. Marc makes long-winded speeches about his favorite topic—building things, such as bridges. But he doesn't make eye contact. He loves numbers, and his head is often in a book.

Marc sticks to routines. He'll eat only certain foods—and even certain brands of those foods.

And yet he is sophisticated in many ways. He has a huge vocabulary, having used large words from a young age. Family members call him their "professor." But he lacks a sense of humor and doesn't understand idioms or figures of speech. Although he was recently enrolled in a special education program that tries to train him in social skills, he isn't making great progress.

Marc is seventeen years old and has never been invited to a birthday party. Throughout his life, he's been bullied. It breaks Joyce's heart.

Joyce explained that being "different" naturally frustrates Marc. She said that the most important thing is to offer love and acceptance.

And that's what she does.

Joyce found out about a special engineering program and spoke to Marc about it. She helped him gather his drawings, and she took photographs of his models. Then the two of them created a portfolio and filled out his application. She's not sure whether Marc will be accepted in the program. If he is, she will offer encouragement. If he isn't, she will be there to support him and to help him apply again the following year.

About a week later, my new friend Barbara told me about her

niece, Lucy. Barbara's brother had died when Lucy was young, and Lucy's mom had remarried. It hadn't been an easy childhood for Lucy. Her stepfather was distant, and her parents largely cut themselves off from Lucy's family. A shy child, Lucy grew up feeling isolated and started to withdraw.

On one occasion, Barbara told Lucy's mother that the child needed encouragement. Lucy liked to draw, and Barbara offered to pay for art lessons. Lucy's mom interpreted Barbara's offer as criticism and told her to back off. Unfortunately, their conversation caught Lucy in the middle—between her mother and her aunt. The tension was too great for Lucy to deal with, and she told her aunt Barbara that things would be easier at home if she didn't "interfere." Barbara explained to Lucy that she would always be her advocate.

Over the next years, there was little contact between them, although Barbara and Lucy saw each other at family events, and the connection between them stayed strong. They enjoyed catching up. Lucy remained withdrawn, but she continued to find refuge in her art. When Lucy was in her late teens, she ran into Barbara at the mall. They had a coffee, and the time flew. "I'd love to see some of your drawings," Barbara told her niece. Lucy promised to mail her a few.

When an envelope with about twenty pictures arrived a week later, Barbara was, in her own words, "blown away." The pictures were cartoons—beautifully executed. Some of the captions were very funny, in a wise way.

Barbara phoned Lucy and asked if she could send a few of the illustrations to a friend who worked as a magazine editor. "I guess so," Lucy said, but she wasn't convinced that her work was anything special. Barbara said she disagreed—she thought they were wonderful.

The editor thought they were wonderful, too. That was about five years ago. Today, Lucy is a successful illustrator whose work appears internationally in magazines and books. She has moved into her own apartment, her self-confidence has gradually grown, and she and Barbara have become close again.

Joyce's and Barbara's stories brought home cherished memories of my Aunts Sylvia, Ann, and Lois. These three women were role models, but they were also friends. They were there at happy times in my life, but also at low points—when I needed advice, comfort, and reassurance.

Who knows? I wondered, after thinking about my own aunts and me, about Joyce and Marc, and about Barbara and Lucy. Maybe that fairy grandmother from childhood stories is really a favorite aunt.

More Good News Stories

At our lowest point, we are often lifted up. A person arrives, a path appears, a light shines in the darkness, or a hand reaches out to guide us in a time of struggle. Here are some stories of acts of kindness and courage that I recently read or heard about.

ACROSS THE FINISH LINE

In 2012, Arden McMath collapsed from exhaustion during the 3,200-meter finals of the Ohio State track and field championships, just meters from the finish line. Rather than run by her, her seventeen-year-old opponent Meghan Vogel stopped to help Arden to her feet. She then carried the fallen runner to the end of the track, where she guided her across the finish line—ahead of herself. (From the *Huffington Post*, June 5, 2012; and *Reader's Digest* magazine, December 2012)

THE BEST REWARD—A BEAUTIFUL SMILE

"MY HAPPINESS IS MY SIGHT," says Cassy Rivera, a Brooklyn mother whose vision was restored in a risky surgery. "Now I can see people laughing and saying 'thank you' to me."

The once-blind mom shows her gratitude by giving to the poor—even though she's poor herself. She buys toys for homeless children and hands out transit passes to those who need them. Her reward is seeing people smile and laugh.

Completely blind until a few years ago, Cassy "couldn't do anything." But in 2009, a specialist was able to restore her vision with an extraordinary procedure. Today, although her inconsistent vision bars her from working, she makes a point of saving fifty dollars a month from her modest disability check to buy gifts for the needy. Before Christmas, she hands out toys and candy canes to families in need.

Cassy is still at risk of again losing her sight, but her outlook remains bright. "When I couldn't see, I couldn't do anything," she explains. "Now," she says with a smile, "I will never, ever, ever stop loving and giving." (From the New York *Daily News*, December 24, 2009)

SINGING WITH SOMEONE ELSE'S LUNGS

CHARITY SUNSHINE TILLEMANN-DICK sings opera with someone else's lungs. The American-born soprano and recipient of two double lung transplants has performed across the United States, Europe, and Asia.

Ever since she was a young girl, Charity was determined to sing. But her precious lungs began to fail her by age twenty. She developed idiopathic pulmonary hypertension, a condition in which oxygen isn't properly absorbed by the body and forces the heart to work overtime.

After receiving her diagnosis in 2004, Charity served as the national spokesperson for the Pulmonary Hypertension Association. In September 2009, Charity received a double lung transplant. Following complications from rejection, she received a second double lung transplant in January 2012. She hoped her voice would be saved and, against all odds, it was.

Today, Charity speaks at events to raise awareness of her disease and to promote organ donation. "Life isn't just about avoiding death," she tells her audience. "It's about living." She takes voice lessons and composes music. And she continues to perform— better than ever, she says—thanks to the lungs of a middle-aged Honduran woman. (From the *Washington Post*, May 27, 2013; CBS News, June 13, 2012; and http://www.ted.com/talks/ charity_tillemann_dick_singing_after_a_double_lung_transplant)

SOMEBODY LOVES YOU

THE 9 NANAS IS A GROUP OF WOMEN devoted to anonymously helping the less fortunate. Every morning in West Tennessee, a person in need receives a freshly baked pound cake on the stoop of his or her door. Attached to the cake is a note, courtesy of the "Nanas," which reads, "Somebody loves you."

For three decades, the women's good deeds went undetected. It was only when one of the husbands started noticing extra mileage on the car that the women were caught out. So the women told their husbands—who then offered to help. Today, the 9 Nanas sneak into the commercial kitchen of a restaurant owned by one of their sons, then leave before the staff come in. (From the *Daily Mail*, June 22, 2012; and *Reader's Digest* magazine, December 2012.)

TEACHING A MESSAGE OF KINDNESS

AFTER A VIDEO of seventh-graders bullying Karen Klein went viral, some thirty thousand people from eighty-four countries donated more than $700,000 to the sixty-eight-year-old bus monitor. The New York State woman had been tormented with insults and threats by four boys during a school bus run.

The fund in support of Klein was conceived by a Toronto man whose goal was to send her on a luxury vacation. But the donations poured in, and eventually Klein became a symbol of the anti-bullying movement. After receiving her check, the former bus driver and monitor started an anti-bullying foundation, which promotes a message of kindness. "When you're an adult and you get bullied, that's one thing," Klein said. "I can handle it. But children can't. It sticks with them forever, and I hope it stops." (From the *Toronto Star*, September 11, 2012; and *Reader's Digest* magazine, December 2012)

THE RIGHT THING TO DO

ON A SATURDAY EVENING in Toronto in 2013, Tom Dillon and his family were heading home from the funeral of Tom's nephew. Arriving at the subway station, they saw a crowd in "absolute panic." A young man had fallen off the platform—apparently after suffering a seizure—smashing his head into the tracks. Nobody was moving, but Tom knew what had to be done and immediately jumped down to the tracks. "That wasn't a problem," he later said, "but getting the boy up was. He was like a dead weight." When Tom's twenty-four-year-old daughter, Kaitie, saw her dad struggling, she jumped in to help.

Tom and Kaitie managed to hoist the young man up and climb back onto the platform before the subway train entered the station. Tom's wife, Terri, along with a student nurse, tried to stop the bleeding. A teenage boy took the shirt off his back to put pressure on the wounds.

Within minutes, first responders arrived to take the young man to the hospital. The Dillon family then took the subway home in blood-soaked clothing. Police said that they were heroic, but Tom said that what he and his family did was simply "the right thing," adding, "I picked a boy up that fell down. It was better to be a firefighter for ten minutes than to have nightmares for the rest of my life." (From the *Toronto Star*, April 25, 2013)

PART FIVE
Kindness and Comfort

And be kind to one another, tenderhearted, forgiving one another,
even as God in Christ forgave you.
    —Ephesians 4:32

As each one has received a gift, minister it to one another, as good
stewards of the manifold grace of God.
    —1 Peter 4:10

Do not forget to entertain strangers, for by so doing some have
unwittingly entertained angels.
    —Hebrews 13:2

Love suffers long and is kind; love does not envy; love does not
    parade itself, is not puffed up;
does not behave rudely, does not seek its own, is not provoked,
    thinks no evil;
does not rejoice in iniquity, but rejoices in the truth;
bears all things, believes all things, hopes all things, endures all
    things.
    —1 Corinthians 13:4–7

When a man's ways please the Lord, He makes even his enemies
to be at peace with him.
    —Proverbs 16:7

WE MAKE A LIFE BY WHAT WE GIVE

Always try to be a little kinder than is necessary.

—J.M. Barrie

Kind hearts are the gardens, Kind thoughts are the roots, Kind words are the flowers, Kind deeds are the fruits. Take care of your garden, And keep out the weeds, Fill it with sunshine, Kind words, and Kind deeds.

—Henry Wadsworth Longfellow

You cannot do a kindness too soon, for you never know how soon it will be too late.

—Ralph Waldo Emerson

Remember there's no such thing as a small act of kindness. Every act creates a ripple with no logical end.

—Scott Adams

Cure sometimes, treat often, comfort always.

—Hippocrates

The closest thing to being cared for is to care for someone else.

—Carson McCullers

We are not put on this earth to see through one another. We are put on this earth to see one another through.

—Gloria Vanderbilt

No act of kindness, however small, is ever wasted.

—Aesop

We make a living by what we get. We make a life by what we give.

—Winston Churchill

Never lose a chance of saying a kind word.

—William Makepeace Thackeray

The Real Spirit of Christmas

Lois Simpson

A stressful time in a stressful year changed a mother's view on what children really need in life.

The year was 1978. My marriage had just ended, and I found myself a single mom with four kids—aged six months and two, eight, and ten years. In previous years, I used to begin buying Christmas gifts in early September and, by the time December rolled around, had several for each child. The living room would be packed with brightly wrapped packages and colorful bows. The morning of December 25 would invariably find me sleep-deprived after having burned the candle at both ends—wrapping presents, fussing over the tree, and making sure everything, on the surface, was picture perfect. I say "on the surface" because the tension of my marriage hung in the air like a heavy cloud, ready to break.

But now my marriage had fallen apart and I found myself a broke single mom, lucky to have five or ten dollars to spare for each child. In previous years, I had gone to the local Christmas tree farm to pick out the fullest tree. This year, I couldn't afford one.

When I told my mother we weren't going to have a tree, she ordered an artificial one as my Christmas present. It looked a little sad, but I was happy to have it. Mom also promised that she and Dad, who usually spent Christmas at my brother's, would be at my house that year. So things were looking less bleak.

I bought one small gift for each child and, feeling a little sorry for myself, wrapped each on the afternoon before Christmas. After a quiet Christmas Eve dinner, the children disappeared to wrap their own presents. Within half an hour, something wonderful happened. My doorbell rang not once, but three times. First, there were the neighbors from across the road; then my next-door neighbor; and then an older couple I had met at a single-parents' group. They all showed up with arms filled with gifts for the children. I hadn't told any of them I had no money—I was too proud, and too embarrassed.

On Christmas morning, my four kids and I all gathered around our tree. Suddenly I realized that, for the first Christmas in many years, there was a sense of peace in our home. This was the first year the children didn't have to beg their father to get out of bed so they could open their presents. There was no grumbling, there was no whispering, there was no stress.

The children treasured their gifts and I treasured the ones they had made for me at school. Shortly before lunch, my parents arrived with a beautiful turkey and all the trimmings. Along with them was a surprise guest—my beloved "Uncle Paul," a boarder who had lived with my family for nearly fifteen years. He played with the kids. There was only joy and love in our house—and the rare sound of laughter.

After the gifts were opened, my oldest son, John, whispered to me that he had something hidden in the garage. Kathy (my oldest child) and I took the kids out of the living room, and when we returned, John had a big smile on his face. The Christmas before, I had bought a kit for a little red wagon along with wheels and axles, but it had remained in the closet, unassembled. Somehow, John had made private arrangements with an elderly friend of mine. He had gone to my friend's garage, climbed up the rafters of his garage, carried down some wooden boards, and then assembled and painted the little wagon for his younger siblings. When the young children returned to the living room and saw the little red wagon with a big bow on it, they jumped right into it. John pulled them out the front door, down the six steps, and raced up and down the street, pulling them in the wagon behind him.

We had a delicious Christmas dinner, and my parents and Uncle Paul continued the visit after dessert as the family sat around the table and played games. When my children finally went to bed, they were content and felt safe and secure.

On Christmas Day 1978, my children and I found out that some things are much more important than material possessions. Surely a guardian angel orchestrated the events of that joyous day. We learned the true value of the gifts of love, of time, and of being surrounded by caring and sensitive people.

The Kindness of Strangers

David Ross

A stranger's good deed can quickly change our perspective, lift our spirits, and make us stop and count life's blessings.

My nephew was getting married. I'd loved this young man since he was born. He had inherited his mom's kind heart and his dad's sense of responsibility. I have no kids, so his wedding would be particularly meaningful.

Relatives would be flying in from all over. My elderly uncle Red—the last surviving member of his generation—would be there. So would other family members, some young, some frail. There is nothing like a happy family event to look forward to and save up for.

Nor did it hurt that the wedding would take place in Florida—two and a half months into the seemingly endless Canadian winter that I was enduring.

My confirmed plane ticket was in hand and, twenty-four hours before the flight, I printed my boarding pass. I thought it curious that it had no seat assignment.

I'm the sort of person who arrives at the airport early, especially for an international flight. I've been flying for half a century. Along the way, I've learned some tricks—the first one is to pack everything in my carry-on luggage. It was a busy day to be flying—the start of spring break—and a mass of people filled the airport. Near the check-in line, an attendant asked to see everyone's boarding passes. She glanced at my luggage and asked if I'd be checking it. "No," I told her. "I have just carry-on."

"In that case," she said helpfully, "don't wait in the line here. Go directly through customs and immigration. You'll get your seat at the gate."

I did as told and proceeded to customs and immigration, then to the gate to claim my seat.

The attendant there looked weary, and when I showed her my boarding pass and requested a seat assignment, she gave me the grim news. "We're completely full," she said. "You won't get on this plane or probably any other today." I was stunned and explained that I had a confirmed ticket plus a boarding pass. "Sorry," she said crustily. "We always overbook—and today my plane is full." Increasingly upset, I explained the importance of this flight—a family wedding the next day, a booked hotel. She wouldn't bend. "I'll take your name in case until everyone is seated, but really . . . I'm completely booked."

Next, the rows were called, the passengers filed into the plane, and I was left in the waiting area. And then . . . I heard my name! There was one unfilled seat. I was led onto a packed plane and found my spot. I was grateful, to be sure. I was also stressed beyond words.

It was late afternoon when the plane landed at the sunny Fort Lauderdale airport. I had booked myself a hotel near the beach— some Florida sunshine would be a bonus, and the location was near the church. I had done some research and found a train that would take me from the airport to the town I was going to. From there, I'd take a cab—the town seemed small, so I expected it wouldn't be a long taxi ride.

Aboard the train was the usual assortment of passengers— commuters, mostly workmen, coming home from a day on the job, a few students, and some people traveling after perhaps a day of shopping or a visit with friends. As the train pulled closer to my stop, I saw the woman next to me put away a notebook and check her phone messages. Her hair was a little disheveled, her clothes rumpled. I asked if she'd be getting off at my station. "Yes," she told me.

"I'm planning to take a cab to my motel," I explained to her. "Do you know if I'll find one in the station parking lot?"

"Where are you going, honey?" she asked.

"To the beach area," I said. "I'm hoping the cab ride won't be too long—maybe a twenty-dollar ride."

She started to laugh. "Mister, twenty bucks won't even get you to the end of the parking lot. It'll be a lot more than that to where you're headed."

The expression on my face must have registered, and she took out her phone. "I'm calling transit to see what bus will get you there." As she made her call, she took out the notebook from her purse and flipped the pink pages till she found a blank sheet. As she talked, she jotted down numbers—the number of the transit company and the number of the bus I'd need. She tore out the page and gave it to me. I thanked her, and we quickly introduced ourselves. Her name was Meg.

At that point, the train pulled into the station. "Follow me," she said. Outside the station, she waved to a man in a mechanic's suit. We walked toward him. I saw the name "Gary" stitched onto his shirt. "Sweetie!" she said loudly as they approached each other. "This poor guy needs to get to the beach. Do you think we can give him a ride to the 42 bus?"

There was genuine kindness in Meg's voice, and Gary didn't hesitate a moment. "Of course—I know exactly where you're going. You get off at Walgreens drug store—Atlantic and Ocean Boulevard."

A few minutes later, I stepped inside the van. There were knick-knacks hanging at the front and the back and a couple of blankets tossed over the back seat, where I sat. I thanked my new friends again and Gary said, "No worries pal. Maybe someday someone will do a good deed for us." Then he got into gear and headed down the road.

Five minutes later, the Number 42 bus came into view. "Hold on tight," Gary said, as he whirled around a corner to get ahead of the bus. "Honey," Meg warned him, "watch out for the cops." "No problem," he shot back. "We're good."

Then he told me to get out quickly and wave down the bus, which was just behind us. I barely had time to thank them as they shooed me out. I wondered if I even had the correct fare. A young man exited the bus and quietly handed me his all-day pass. "OK if I use this?" I asked the driver as I stepped onboard. "Sure," he smiled.

I double-checked with the driver. "You stop at Walgreens, right?"

"Yes—my last stop." A fellow at the front of the bus told me he'd be getting off there, so I should follow him. We chatted—I told him I was going to a wedding the next evening, and he made suggestions about places to see and where to eat if I had time.

At the last stop, we got out and my new friend wished me well as he turned in the direction opposite to where I was headed. It was dark, and the streets seemed deserted. I approached a woman leaving Walgreens, asked her if she knew where my motel was, and she insisted on walking me there. "I'm passing right by."

The woman who ran the motel had told me that if I arrived late,

I should use a code to get into the gate and would find the key in the door of Room 10. The room was modest but clean, and immediately I crashed. Suddenly I realized how hungry I was. By now it was 9 p.m., and I hadn't eaten since before my 2 p.m. flight. But everything was dark and unfamiliar, and I felt uncomfortable venturing outside in this new place.

"I'll never sleep," I told myself as I hit the sheets. "I'm hungry, stressed out, and overtired."

It was dark when I woke up, but there was a hint of a pink sky. Six a.m. Despite all my worries, I had slept for eight solid hours.

I looked at the nightstand and saw the pink paper that Meg had torn from her notebook—the number of the bus I needed to take, and the phone number of the transit office. Suddenly my mind flashed back to the previous day. I picked up the paper and it finally came to me how kind and generous several strangers had been to a frustrated visitor from Canada.

I was about to toss the pink paper into the garbage but thought I'd save it as a reminder of my unusual day. I folded it in half, and as I did, I saw writing on the reverse side. It appeared to be Meg's budget from the previous month. Among the items on it, with the amounts beside them, were several that caught my eye:

Rent
Gas
Food
Gift for Mrs. M.
Nurse
Train fare (hospital)

There were other items, but those were the first few. I was surprised at how low the rent and food expenses were, and when I saw the items for the nurse and the hospital, I stopped. I had been so preoccupied with my own superficial problem—a plane mix-up—that I hadn't thought about what others were dealing with in their lives. Then I thought about Meg, who had taken a stranger—me—under her wing, with a heart full of warmth. And Gary—who didn't have a clue who I was—simply had said, "Maybe someday someone will do a good deed for us."

For the first time in sixteen hours, things were placed in perspective. My own "stress" seemed trivial, and I was embarrassed by how I had reacted.

I quickly showered, hopped into my shorts, and headed to the ocean, ready to take the day and see the world through new eyes.

When I stepped onto the pristine beach, the sun was still not very high in the sky, and it seemed I was alone at this early hour. There was a pier far away to the north, and another in the distance to the south. And when I looked in between, I saw random footprints scattered everywhere in the sand.

A Perfect Cup of Coffee

Tina Sullivan

**We can apply the "Footprints" message to our everyday lives—
not just in times of hardship.**

I'm often reminded of the beautiful message behind "Footprints
in the Sand." This year, Donna, my mom's oldest and dearest
friend, passed away. Donna had lived a rich, full life, and she
knew that she had received the gift of a good year following her
diagnosis. Shortly before she died, she said to her family, "I've had
my innings. I'm ready."

It was a difficult time for my mom. She and Donna had grown
up together in a small town and were inseparable as kids. They
were each other's maids of honor, and even after they moved to
different cities, they stayed close. Donna and her family had spent
summer vacations at our cottage for as long as I can remember,
and every year, Donna and my mom took a "girls'" vacation.

About a year ago, a woman I work with introduced me to the poem "Footprints in the Sand." I sent a copy of it to my mom, and a few days later, she called to say that it gave her comfort and encouraged her to focus on her happy memories with her friend, to know that the memories would carry her on.

A few months ago, I picked up a copy of a book by Margaret Fishback Powers, the author of the poem. In the book *Footprints: The True Story Behind the Poem That Inspired Millions*, the author talks about her inspiration to write the poem. She shared her life's story, showing how God demonstrated His faithfulness through challenging times. The book also includes letters and recollections from people around the world. A man from Alberta wrote about how the poem had encouraged him to stop worrying about an upcoming surgery and to concentrate on building a positive attitude to help the healing process. A woman from California explained how, during an emotional crisis, the image of footprints in the sand had appeared for a brief moment—and in a flash, she had realized the significance of the poem. Another woman, from Ontario, explained how the poem had provided healing over the years. From Japan, a reader talked about the tsunami that had hit that country so hard, and felt that God had used "Footprints" as a way of reaching out.

But the other day, something happened that made me stop and think about the message of the poem and how we can apply it in our everyday life, not only during times of personal crisis.

My family had gone off on a weekend skiing trip. It was early December, and winter had arrived early. I decided to stay home to catch up on some work. At about six in the evening, the power went off in our neighborhood. The first clue was when the computer screen turned black (so much for catching up on work) and the desk light went out. Then I looked out the window and saw . . . nothing. I looked toward the high-rise apartment building down the street, and every window was dark. After a time, I saw candles and flashlights flicker.

No lights, no stove, no phone, no heat, and no computer. I managed to make myself a sandwich, and at 8:30 p.m., I crawled into bed. Two blankets and one quilt later I was snug. All was well with the world for the next nine hours.

It was well before dawn on a snowy Sunday morning when I made my way into the kitchen and flicked on a light switch. Nothing! Who knew how long this blackout would last?

Everything looks brighter after a cup of coffee, but that wasn't an option. Or perhaps it was. I'm nothing if not resourceful, and within minutes, I was fumbling about the hall closet. I pulled my full-length down-filled coat over my pajamas, then grabbed a scarf and hat and pair of mittens, and finally stepped into my boots. Within minutes, I was walking to the nearest streetcar stop, about ten blocks away. My plan was to go eastward—in the direction of downtown—and ride the streetcar till I saw the first coffee shop that was open.

The streetcars don't run very frequently on Sunday mornings, so I counted myself lucky to wait just fifteen minutes. The sky was just starting to brighten and the driver probably didn't see me waiting until the last moment. As the wheels ground to a sudden stop, I found myself splattered in messy slush. I got on board, shook myself off the best I could, found a seat at the back and, after a few blocks, noticed lights on in the houses. Turning back, I saw that my own neighborhood was still plunged in darkness.

I found some tissues in my coat pocket and started to clean the mess off my face and my glasses. As I removed my mittens, I realized they were an obviously mismatched pair. I also observed that the scarf I had chosen in the darkness was the ratty old thing my teenage daughter couldn't bring herself to part with, despite my urging. There were a few other souls on the streetcar. I imagined they were heading to an early Sunday shift somewhere. Some looked half-asleep. Nobody was smiling.

Twenty minutes later, we were finally heading into a more populated area. It was about seven thirty, and the sun was struggling to make an appearance in the still-gray sky. I spied a first coffee shop—but it was closed. About ten minutes and three lonely-looking coffee shops later, I spotted a place that appeared open. We were now in the heart of downtown, but, on an early Sunday morning, the streets appeared eerily unpopulated.

I left the streetcar and trudged across the wide street through the dirty snow. I thought about my family on the pristine ski slopes—a world away. They were probably enjoying a hearty breakfast of fresh pancakes, crispy bacon, and steaming hot chocolate.

The shop was empty, but I was greeted with the wonderful aroma of just-brewed coffee and fresh baking. I walked up to the counter and was welcomed with a smiling face—the first smile of the morning for me. What a welcome sight! Before ordering, I told the waitress my tale of woe—having no light or heat in my pocket of the city, getting splashed with filthy snow, and feeling totally bedraggled, with my mismatched mittens, my hopeless scarf, and my bright yellow down coat thrown over my flannel pajamas. The waitress flashed another smile and said, "I'm surprised you didn't mention the hat." I reached to my head and discovered I had put on my mother's fur fedora—what my daughter kindly called "retro."

The waitress and I had a good laugh as she poured my coffee. "I've given you an extra large," she said as she handed me the cup, "and added an extra shot of caffeine. I figured you needed it."

I don't think I've ever enjoyed a cup of coffee more. As I sipped it, I thought about the poem I had given my mom. Its message provides comfort in times of loss, sadness, and worry. But it also reminds us about the difference that a friendly face and an everyday act of kindness can make.

This Little Light

Cory Leon

A light of kindness shines in the darkness.

About a year ago, my husband's firm sent him to a conference in Atlanta. I tagged along and, while Tom attended meetings, I explored the city—everything from the stately mansions to the botanical gardens and outstanding museums. I saw the apartment where Margaret Mitchell had written *Gone with the Wind* and visited the inspiring Martin Luther King, Jr., National Historic Site. It was mid-April, and the delicate dogwood blossoms were in glorious bloom.

Tom and I met in the evenings, either at a conference-sponsored event or at one of the little restaurants that had caught my eye during my daytime explorations. It was a memorable few days for us, and I fell in love with the city's charms. We found the locals warm and hospitable, and we decided to stay an extra day so I could show Tom some of the sights and we could celebrate our anniversary. We enjoyed a wonderful candlelit dinner at a fine local restaurant. The atmosphere was romantic, but also a little dark. So when our young waiter presented the bill, he offered Tom a mini-flashlight so he could read it.

"What a great idea," I said. "It certainly would be useful when I walk the dog on those dark New England winter nights."

Without missing a beat, the waiter insisted that I take the light—he'd be able to find another.

IT WASN'T LONG BEFORE DECEMBER CAME AROUND. And on one of those dark New England nights, I found myself driving to a friend's home when, without warning, a whiteout caught me by surprise. The car spun on the slick ice, and I swerved into a ditch. Thankfully, I was fine and able to climb out of the car. But the snow was blinding, and I couldn't find my bearings on the country road. I knew I was about ten minutes from the closest home—my friend's home—but I had lost all sense of direction. I fumbled for my cell phone, but at some point, it must have fallen. Thankfully, my gloves were still in my pocket—and so was something else. It was the little flashlight the waiter had given me. I'd forgotten that I had transferred it to my winter coat.

I touched the switch, and the light immediately glowed. I was amazed at how strong it was and how far I could see, despite the heavy squalls. At once I knew where I was, and where I should be heading. I wondered how strong the battery was, but the little light faithfully led me to my friend's home. And along the way, I found myself singing an old Gospel song that I hadn't thought about for years:

This little light of mine, I'm gonna let it shine.
This little light of mine, I'm gonna let it shine.
This little light of mine, I'm gonna let it shine.
Let it shine, let it shine, let it shine.

I spent the night at my friend's home, and the next day, the local garage retrieved the car—no real damage. For several days, I continued to hum the song that, along with the little flashlight, had guided me to my destination. Then I decided to find out about the song's history. I learned that it had been written in about 1920 by a teacher named Harry Dixon Loes. Some sources say it's based on Matthew 5:16: "Let your light so shine before men, that they may see your good works and glorify your Father in heaven."

What a beautiful message. What a beautiful song. And what a beautiful and unexpected gift I had been given eight months earlier, by a young waiter in Atlanta.

Look After Your Kids

Andrea Palmer

Days, weeks, even years later, we may come to realize that criticism was concern. If people see children doing things that are dangerous, they are often afraid to get involved. God is always with us. He will never forsake us, but He doesn't expect us to be foolish or fearless.

It was the kids' first time in a large city, and my husband's and my first visit in more than ten years. We were fascinated by the tall buildings, overwhelmed by the crush of people everywhere, and exhausted just looking at the endless shops and choices of restaurants. Living all our lives in a town of under a thousand people, we could have been on another planet and not in the center of a city of about three million.

We live in Huron County in Ontario and have always considered ourselves lucky to be there. We have Lake Huron—sometimes called "the lake that thinks it's an ocean," because of its crashing waves. We never tire of the rolling hills of the countryside. The lush farms provide the sweetest corn and the biggest zucchini. Our neighbors are the best in the world—no question about it. And our two kids, ten-year-old Hank and seven-year-old Tina, are content to play outside every season, especially in winter—thanks to the natural "skating rink" in our backyard.

We often shop in nearby Goderich, which calls itself "the prettiest town in Canada." And though I haven't of course been to every town in the country—or even in Huron County—I can't imagine a prettier place or a friendlier one.

But now we were in Toronto. My childhood friend Mary Pat, who has an important job at a downtown insurance company, had called to say she'd be away for a few days. "Andrea," she said, "you can have my place to yourselves. Bring Glenn and the children. Toronto is a safe city, and you'll have a great time." We thought it would be a good experience for our kids—we'd take them to all the popular attractions, including the zoo, the museum, and of course the Hockey Hall of Fame.

It was a steamy late-August day, our first full day in the city, and we were on our way to the CN Tower and then a Major League Baseball game—the choice of my oldest "kid," my husband, Glenn. We had taken the subway to Union Station from the apartment. That was an experience for all of us, but what I noticed most was that people didn't smile much. Were they busy thinking about work? How sad.

As we walked up the stairs of the station to Front Street, our eyes were drawn upward to all the skyscrapers. The one across the street was a golden building that sparkled in the midmorning sunlight. Behind it were towers of various heights and shapes. It was dazzling. It also amused me that the locals, as they pounded the pavement, were oblivious to these urban wonders. Back home, I never take the landscape for granted. I thank God daily for the beauty He provides. Maybe it's different in the city.

Everyone seemed to be in a great hurry, but I managed to stop a woman and ask her where the CN Tower was. She looked a little amused as she pointed toward the structure that seemed high enough to pierce the clouds. I'm sure she was thinking, *It's pretty obvious where it is, isn't it?*

The four of us hurried along Front Street. Vendors were selling hotdogs, and sightseeing buses lined the street outside a large hotel. We were about two blocks from the tower, and the kids were darting back and forth—in front of us and then behind us—as some new wonder caught their attention. They were intrigued by everything from the bumper-to-bumper traffic to the smart outfits that some of the young men and women sported. Although there were other tourists walking toward the tower, I'm sure we stood out as a bunch of hicks.

A woman brushed by me and turned in my direction. I thought

she was going to apologize for nearly knocking me down, but instead, she glanced at me critically and snapped, pointedly, "Look after your kids!" There was something judgmental in her voice, and I was immediately put off by her tone. I turned around, and Tina and Hank were several paces behind Glenn and me, their necks tilted far back as they gazed upward at the tower. "Come on guys," I called, and right away they caught up with us.

"What was that all about, honey?" Glenn asked.

"I have no idea," I told him. "But that woman"—I looked ahead and she was already out of sight—"had the nerve to tell me to look after our kids. For goodness' sake, they were right behind us. Who does she think she is, telling me to look after our own children?"

The more I thought about it, the more annoyed I became. *She was so arrogant!* I thought. *Does she think I'm a bad parent? She knows nothing about me!*

The visit to the tower was a success. We couldn't have asked for a clearer day, and we looked across Lake Ontario to Niagara Falls and far beyond. The baseball game was next on the agenda. The sunshine continued, the dome stayed open and, best of all, the home team Blue Jays won.

The rest of our trip was equally successful, with visits to all the planned places—and, of course, lots of clothing stores and restaurants. I think we liked the many different neighborhoods best of all. We had never seen anything like Chinatown—and I have to say that the food at an authentic Chinese restaurant was totally different from our experience at the China Palace back home.

By the fourth and last day of our trip, we felt almost at home in the big city. The kids stayed within sight—I insisted on it. But the remarks of that stranger continued to bother me, and I continued to stew over that rude encounter on the first day of our visit. How could anyone think I was an unfit parent? Who would have the nerve to tell me to look after my own children?

We were a little sorry to say good-bye to Toronto, but now it was Saturday and time to return to small-town Ontario. Once back, we barely had time to recover from our mini-holiday. The kids were about to start school again after the summer holiday.

Once Tina and Hank climbed into the yellow school bus and I waved them good-bye, I headed back into the house. There was still more laundry to do, but first I put on the kettle for my morning tea. No sooner had the water come to a boil than I heard a knock at the door. I should have known. My oldest friend and dearest neighbor, Bonnie, was greeting me with a basket of fresh blueberry muffins. (You'll find the recipe for Bonnie's famous Huron County Blueberry Muffins on page 227.)

"Oh, honey," she said as she grabbed a chair. "I'm dying to hear about your big-city adventure."

So I started to fill her in on everything we had seen—from the latest styles to the strange new foods to the high cost of everything. I told her about the subways and the streetcars, the crowds at the ball park, the wonders of the Royal Ontario Museum. "It was a wonderful experience for the kids," I explained, "and for us, too, it couldn't have been a better trip—except for one upsetting experience."

"Oh?" Bonnie asked as she poured herself a cup of tea. "What happened?"

I started to tell her about our first full day, when we were walking to the CN Tower. How a total stranger, in a smart business suit, had had the audacity to tell me to look after my kids. "Heck, Bonnie," I said as I shook my head, "I'll bet she didn't even have children herself. Do you believe the nerve of some people?"

Bonnie took a sip of tea and then paused. I knew what that meant. She was carefully choosing her words.

After about two minutes, she began. "Andrea, dear," she asked. "Where were the kids when that woman spoke to you?"

"Just a few steps behind us," I answered. "They didn't want to miss a thing."

"Honey," Bonnie continued. "Don't take this the wrong way, please. But bad things do happen everywhere—in big cities and even in small towns. That woman probably knew you were visitors and not familiar with the city. I think, really, she meant well. Even though she was brusque, she was reminding you to be careful."

Bonnie has always been wise—and frank—and that's why I love her dearly. Now, for the first time since my encounter on

Front Street, I thought things through from a different perspective. Over the past few days, I had stewed over that woman's attitude—she was critical, arrogant, judgmental, and obnoxious. And then, in an instant, I suddenly understood that none of those traits mattered. Only one thing counted. And it was that a perfect stranger had stopped for a moment and taken the time and the trouble to—yes—look after my kids.

On a Hot Day in August

Emma Bell

"Coincidence is God's way of remaining anonymous."
—Albert Einstein

I'm in my late seventies and have lived in small-town Ontario most of my life. I was a teacher for many years, and I stay in touch with some of my former students, a few of whom live abroad. About two years ago, after my husband passed away, I moved to the picturesque city of Stratford.

In the warmer months, I get around Stratford on my bicycle. I have a couple of old friends who live nearby, and I've made some new acquaintances at church.

Once a month, I take the train from Stratford to Toronto to see a medical specialist. It's a pleasant ride of about two and a half hours. I usually read or knit on the train, and the time passes quickly. I leave in the morning, catching the 8:35 train and arriving by eleven. My appointment is for 2 p.m., so I get something to eat before making my way to the doctor's office. After my appointment, I sometimes shop for clothes or certain groceries that I can't find at home. Once in a while, I visit briefly with a friend. I catch the 5:30 p.m. return train and am home by eight.

A year ago last August, as I prepared for my regular Thursday trip, a Toronto friend called to caution me about the extreme weather there. The city was experiencing record heat—the temperature was expected to reach a hundred degrees—and she thought I should cancel my appointment. I told her I'd be fine.

On the train I seated myself next to a man who also boarded in Stratford. He was younger than I, though not by much. He was working on his computer, so I took out my book and began to read.

I find it interesting that some voices carry more loudly than others, and about six rows in front of me a chap seemed to be telling his unfortunate seatmate his entire life story. Just as the man was explaining what had happened to a $50,000 investment, I excused myself to freshen up. When I returned, the man beside me filled me in on the details I had missed. We shared a good laugh and both of us agreed that we were lucky to be sitting where we were and not beside the loudmouth.

Before long, my seatmate and I were exchanging stories—in quiet tones—about our own lives, which were decidedly less interesting. He was an accountant, he lived in Toronto, and his name was Marc. I introduced myself as Emma, explaining I was named after the Jane Austen heroine, and told him that, after retiring, I had written a cookbook on desserts. Our conversation soon turned to food.

When I told Marc about my long day ahead, he reminded me to keep cool and not venture out of Toronto's air-conditioned "underground city." I told him I'd be all right—my doctor was only a short walk from the Bathurst Street subway station. He looked at his computer and said that the temperature had now passed a hundred degrees.

I told Marc he should stay out of the heat, too. He said he had a meeting downtown later in the day and hoped it would cool off by then.

The last portion of the trip flew by. I was sorry we hadn't introduced ourselves earlier, but glad that we struck up a conversation when we did. As the train pulled in to Toronto, we exchanged good-byes and said we hoped we'd meet again. And his parting words were for me to keep cool.

I left Toronto's Union Station and headed to a nearby market. The heat was oppressive. I don't recall a day so hot and unpleasant. I picked up my favorite cookies—an English brand that I can't find in Stratford—and stopped for a coffee. I thought I'd have lunch downtown before heading to my appointment.

The doctor was running late, but I was happy to wait in his

air-conditioned reception room. He saw me at about two thirty and the appointment went well. He too warned me to keep out of the heat.

It was after three thirty when I left the doctor's office. I opened the door of his building and was greeted by a blast of heat. It was overpowering, and I decided to make my way to Union Station as quickly as possible and wait in an air-conditioned coffee shop till departure time.

It was just a block to the Bathurst Street subway station, but I felt drained when I got there. I walked down the stairs to the platform and headed for the eastbound subway, which I would ride for two stops. Then, at the St. George station, I would connect to another subway line. I knew the routine well. The air was still and the station crowded with people all looking weary from the heat. The subway arrived and, to everyone's misery, the air-conditioning system was down. A gentleman offered me his seat but I politely declined—I had only two stations. By the time we arrived at St. George, however, I was feeling exhausted, dizzy, and disoriented. The stifling heat had completely knocked the wind out of my sails.

When you get off the subway at St. George, you have to walk down a flight of stairs and wait for a southbound train to Union Station. But after I exited the subway, instead of going down the stairs, I simply crossed the platform. In other words, I was waiting for a subway that would take me west, not south—right back to where I had come from. The heat grew more oppressive, and I felt more confused, and then the subway pulled in. But before I boarded it, I heard a voice calling my name. Coming toward me was a familiar-looking man. "Emma," he said. "I'm Marc. We met this morning, on the train from Stratford."

There was an empty bench on the subway platform, and Marc guided me to it.

"Are you all right?" he asked.

"I don't think so," I said hesitantly.

"I was worried when I saw you," he said. "I knew you had to go back to Stratford today, but you were waiting for the wrong subway."

He explained that he was heading home after his appointment and wasn't rushing to go anywhere. He suggested we have a glass of water or iced tea while I regained my composure.

We went to a nearby diner, and by the time I had finished my glass of water, I felt fine. I thanked him and told him I'd be on my way. But as we walked along the street, he called a cab, handed the driver a twenty-dollar bill, and told him to take me to Union Station.

Since that time, I've been back and forth to Toronto about fifteen times but have never again seen Marc. A few months ago, a friend told me about a book she had read. It was about Arctic explorers, mountaineers, and aviators who claimed to have experienced the presence of a helper or guardian who guided them through snowstorms, fatigue, or hypothermia. My friend asked if I believed such a presence existed during such traumatic times.

Yes, I told her. I certainly did.

It Only Takes a Moment

Janet Stein

A special song—or poem—can bring back loving memories and provide comfort.

Bob and I were childhood sweethearts—in fact, we remained sweethearts for our entire marriage—over forty years—until he passed away quite suddenly. We weren't blessed with children, but our life was rich and fulfilling. Our careers took different paths. Bob was a teacher, I was a nurse. We were both active in our church, shared a love of the theater, and enjoyed traveling, taking long weekend drives, no matter the weather.

On our first date, we saw the musical *Hello, Dolly!* There's a beautiful song that comes near the end of the show. After a series of mishaps and adventures, the young couple finally realize how much in love they are with each other and sing "It Only Takes a Moment." That became our song, and we listened to it often. Years later, we were delighted when the song was introduced to a new generation in the animated movie *WALL-E*, about a lovesick robot.

When Bob and I retired, we looked forward to spending time in our garden, traveling when we could, and enjoying the books we had always been too busy to read. It was not to be. Just a few months after we hung up our hats, Bob was diagnosed with pancreatic cancer. He died a few months later.

Friends tried to comfort me as best they could, but I went around in a haze. I found myself spending my days going from coffee shop to coffee shop, with the occasional stop at a library. I couldn't bear to be home alone. I felt sad, of course, but aimless too. My doctor suggested I have some grief counseling, but I didn't have the interest, or the energy.

Sometimes, on my rounds of the local coffee shops, I'd strike up a conversation with a stranger. I felt it easier to talk to people I didn't know than to my friends. I'd talk about Bob and how kind he was. His students loved him, and I'd take a letter or two out of my purse to show to my coffee companion. "Your husband taught me a love of language that lasted far more than a semester. It influenced my life in wonderful ways, and I will forever be grateful." Some strangers were kind, but mostly they humored an old lady and, after a few minutes of my rambling, politely told me they had to get back to work or to school.

I found it harder and harder to get out of bed. I think the word that best described me was *blasé*. Bob and I both enjoyed good food. I was the everyday cook, and he made the gourmet meals on weekends. Depending on the most recent cookbook that caught his eye, we'd be dining in southwestern France, northern Africa, the Middle East, or Thailand. Just before he took ill, he discovered the joys of vegetarian dishes. Weekends were always an adventure in cuisines. Friends dropped hints for invitations at holiday time. But after Bob died, I couldn't be bothered with more than a bowl of cereal for breakfast, a bowl of soup for lunch, and something convenient from the supermarket for dinner—often a rotisserie chicken with overcooked vegetables.

I often ignored the telephone, especially when I recognized the number as belonging to some relative or friend who no doubt wanted to invite me for lunch and give me a pep talk. But one afternoon, when I was probably at my lowest point, the phone rang and I answered it. On the other end of the line was the friendly voice of my dentist's receptionist, reminding me of my semi-annual appointment with the hygienist the next day. "Sure, I'll see you then," I told her. The office was at the other end of town—I had to take the subway to get there. *Maybe I'll try out a coffee shop in that neighborhood,* I told myself.

The next day, after my oatmeal and my other morning routines, I set out for the dentist. I walked the three blocks to the subway station and then headed down the stairs. There was the usual hum of trains and chatter, but over the noise, I heard music—a violin. That wasn't unusual, because you often find musicians playing in our subway stations. The city holds auditions, and accordionists, keyboard players, violinists, and other musicians are licensed to perform in different stations and collect coins in return for the pleasure they bring commuters. There was something about the tune I heard. I couldn't quite place it, but it grew clearer and clearer as I got closer to the ticket booth. A young violinist—in his twenties, I imagine—was playing his fiddle with great gusto. And as I approached him, he flashed a smile. Immediately, it clicked! He was fiddling the song that had been so special to Bob and me, "It Only Takes a Moment." I was so surprised that I walked right by him, through the turnstile, and boarded my train.

Later, at the dentist's, where Bob and I had been patients for years, Dr. Warren, his hygienist, and his receptionist all expressed their condolences. The cleaning went smoothly, I booked my next appointment, and instead of stopping in at the local coffee shop, I did something I hadn't done in months: I went to the market nearby and bought a fresh chicken, some decent vegetables, and a slice of my favorite pie. Then I headed to the subway and back home.

The half-hour trip was uneventful. When I exited the train and walked toward the escalator, I heard the faint sounds of a violin. *Ah,* I thought to myself. *I must put a dollar or two inside the violinist's open case this time.* The music grew louder and the song was suddenly recognizable. Again, "It Only Takes a Moment." *Is it a coincidence?* I wondered. *Or is it the only song the man knows?*

I passed through the turnstile, reached into my purse for some coins to toss into the violin case. When I looked upward, the musician, smiling broadly, was playing the song with even greater verve than the first time. Again, he flashed me a smile. As his bow traveled up and down the violin strings, there wasn't just a twinkle in the young man's eyes. I could swear he winked as I walked by him.

Suddenly, my heart was lighter than it had been in many months.

Comfort Foods

Bonnie Thompson

A homemade dish, prepared with love, is a gift of pure kindness.

When my friend Andrea Palmer asked if I would like to write a story for this collection, I hesitated. Although I'm a great fan of the poem "Footprints in the Sand," I told her, "I'm not much of a writer." Together we talked about the theme of the book—about how, in times of difficulty, a relative, a friend, a stranger, or some higher power helps us through a difficult time. "Bonnie," Andrea said, "you're the one who's always there with cookies, or a casserole, or some other comfort food." She then suggested I share some of my recipes. So here they are—and I hope you prepare them to bring comfort to others . . . and to yourself, too.

Cabbage Soup

This recipe also works as a main-course stew. You'll need a large, heavy pot and lots of time to cut up the vegetables.

2 tablespoons vegetable oil
1 pound medium ground beef
1 medium onion, diced
½ cup diced celery
½ green pepper, diced
2 teaspoons salt (or to taste)
½ teaspoon pepper
½ teaspoon paprika
1 (28 ounce) can of stewing tomatoes, chopped roughly
    (or a can of diced tomatoes)
2 (5 ounce) cans of tomato paste (or prepared tomato sauce)
4 cups hot water
2 chili peppers or a dash of cayenne pepper (optional)
2 cups diced potatoes
1 cup diced carrots
3 tablespoons chopped parsley
6 cups coarsely chopped cabbage
1 cup beef stock (optional)

In a large pot, heat the oil. Sauté the ground beef (breaking it up), onion, celery, and green pepper until the meat is browned.

Add all the other ingredients except the cabbage and optional beef stock.

Simmer, uncovered, for 1 hour.

Remove the chili peppers (if used), add the cabbage, and simmer, covered, until the cabbage is tender (check after 15 minutes).

The soup should be quite thick. You can add water or beef stock if you prefer a thinner soup.

Old-Fashioned Meat Loaf

Is there any food more comforting than meat loaf—especially when served with mashed potatoes? This recipe is my standby. You'll need a large bowl for the meat mixture, a small one for the sauce, and an 8 x 4 x 4-inch loaf pan. Preheat oven to 350°F.

For the meat loaf:

1½ pounds lean (not extra-lean) ground beef
   (or ground turkey)
1 slice bread, broken into small pieces
1 egg
1 small onion, finely chopped
1 teaspoon salt
¼ teaspoon pepper
4 tablespoons ketchup or chili sauce
⅔ cup whole milk or half-and-half cream

For the sauce:
4 tablespoons apple cider vinegar
2–4 tablespoons dark brown sugar (to taste)
½ cup ketchup

Combine the meat loaf ingredients in a large bowl and transfer into the loaf pan. Flatten the top of the mixture.

Combine the sauce ingredients in a small bowl and pour over the top and sides of the meat loaf.

Bake at 350°F for one hour. Check for doneness, and continue baking for another 15 minutes if required.

Pure Cheesecake

This cheesecake has brought comfort to family and friends over many years. Yes, it's rich—but sometimes that's just what we need. I've cut back on the calories by omitting a crust—nobody misses it. The cake freezes well. I like to freeze individual slices using plastic wrap—and bring out a couple of slices when the occasion arises. The cake is perfect on its own, though you may wish to serve slightly sweetened strawberries or raspberries on the side.

You'll need a 9-inch springform pan and a stand mixer or food processor with a strong motor. (A trusty blender will work, too.)

For the cake:
24 ounces (three 8-ounce packages) cream cheese

4 large eggs
1 cup granulated sugar
1 teaspoon vanilla

For the topping:
2 cups (1 pint) sour cream (not low fat)
¾ cup granulated sugar

In a large bowl, combine the cream cheese, eggs, 1 cup granulated sugar, and vanilla.

Beat at medium speed for 20–25 minutes.

Place the cheese mixture in a lightly buttered 9-inch springform pan. Bake 40 minutes at 325°F.

Cool the cake in the pan for 35 minutes.

While the cake is cooling, beat the sour cream and ¾ cup granulated sugar in a small bowl for 10 minutes.

Pour the sour cream mixture over the top of the cooked cake.

Bake for 15 minutes at 400°F. Watch carefully. It should brown *very* slightly on top. (If it doesn't brown in 15 minutes, leave it in the oven, checking carefully, for another 5 minutes.)

Refrigerate the cheesecake in the springform pan overnight.

Huron County Blueberry Muffins

I like to celebrate the arrival of blueberry season with these not-too-sweet, berry-packed muffins. Preheat oven to 350°F. You'll need two large bowls, a beater, and a muffin tin lined with twelve paper or foil cups.

1½ cups white flour
½ teaspoon baking soda
1 teaspoon baking powder
¼ teaspoon salt
⅓ cup light honey
¼ cup unsalted butter
½ teaspoon fresh lemon rind
⅓ cup milk
1 large egg
2 tablespoons fresh lemon juice
1½ cups fresh blueberries

In a large bowl, sift together the flour, baking soda, baking powder, and salt. Make a well in the center of the dry ingredients.

In a small saucepan, melt the light honey and butter and allow to cool. Transfer to another large bowl.

Add all remaining ingredients except the berries to the melted honey and butter. Pour this mixture into the well of the dry ingredients, and stir gently—till just blended.

Add the blueberries gradually, carefully folding them in.

Fill the muffin cups about ⅔ full. (I use an ice cream scoop.)

Bake 30–35 minutes until an inserted toothpick comes out clean.

Cool the muffins in the tin for about 5 minutes before removing.

Elijah's Cup

Ellyn Jacoby

A message bringing hope may arrive at an unexpected time, in an unexpected way.

Passover is the holiday I most look forward to. It is a time when our loved ones gather together, when even the busiest of the adults and children find time to sit around the table and read the Haggadah—the book that sets out the order of the evening. It also gives me a chance to be creative in the kitchen, because this is the holiday when we eat nothing with leavening. Everything from the traditional chicken soup with matzo balls to a nut cake is made without flour. Preparation takes several days, and the kitchen is redolent with wonderful aromas.

But Passover is much more than food. Every year, several generations of our family, along with dear friends, have celebrated this special holiday around our large dining room table. Together we observe a joyous festival that Jewish people all over the world have celebrated for thousands of years. We celebrate our freedom, when our ancestors left Egypt and slavery and began their journey to the Promised Land. We also acknowledge the injustices that people around the world face today.

For those not familiar with the Passover Seder, it is led by an elder member of the family, though everyone who attends participates. The Seder also includes special activities to hold the interest of children.

This year's Seder was a difficult one for me. For many years, my mom and I had shared a tradition of preparing the foods together. This would be my first Passover since Mom had passed away. It wouldn't be the same, and I knew I would have trouble getting through it. Although I would prepare everyone's favorite flourless chocolate cake, I was relieved that my daughter and daughter-in-law offered to do most of the preparation this year. This would be the first Seder in nearly twenty years with only three generations represented.

Adding to my sadness, my husband and I were going through a tough period. We had always felt our marriage had a good foundation, but now it seemed that the foundation was crumbling. Let me simply say there were many problems, and I didn't know if we could work them out.

For the Seder, my grandchildren and I had prepared the Seder plate. There are several symbolic foods on this large, round platter, including a few sprigs of parsley, symbolizing the beginning of springtime and representing hope and renewal; and two matzos—flat, unleavened bread—in a folded napkin, representing the loaves of bread that did not have time to rise when our ancestors fled Egypt.

The Seder begins with several prayers and songs, and we take turns reading from our books. We tell the story of Passover—from the bitterness of slavery to the struggle for freedom. The youngest member reads four questions—asking why this night is different from other nights. And another person at the table answers the questions, explaining the reasons.

After our prayers and songs, we begin our meal. Chicken soup, pot roast with vegetables, a green salad, and dessert are traditional in our home. Then, at the end of the meal, we pour a cup of wine for the prophet Elijah. At each table, there is the extra cup of wine (or juice) and one remaining matzo. At this point in the Seder, we open the door and say, "Let all who are hungry, come eat. We now welcome Elijah, beloved guest at our Seder, as we rise." As we stand, we pray that Elijah, the messenger of peace, will enter our homes, lift our spirits, and bring hope to our hearts.

Since I was a young girl, my mother and I had shared the tradition of opening the door for the prophet. This year, I walked alone to the door. As I let in the fresh springtime air, I looked upward at the stars and the brilliant full moon. My mom and I had always waited outside for a few extra moments, counting the stars and tightly grasping each other's hand. I started to count the stars, but as I began, I wiped a tear from my eye. After more than thirty years of what seemed like a good marriage, I didn't know what lay ahead for me. Would we make it to the finish line? Who knew? I reached into my pocket for a tissue, and as I did, something on the porch caught my eye. There lay a piece of paper, weighted down by a stone, its corners fluttering in the gentle wind. *How odd,* I thought, as I bent down to pick it up.

Our family and guests were as curious as I was as I walked back to the table, holding the square paper in my hand. I set it down at my place, and read the one word that was written on it: "Shalom." In Hebrew, *shalom* means many things, including "peace be yours" and "welcome home."

Everyone had a different theory about the unexpected message. My granddaughter thought it was a prank that her eight-year-old brother was playing. But from the expression on his face, I knew he was innocent. My oldest friend thought that one of our neighbors, perhaps the new couple across the road, had placed the message as a greeting. And my son-in-law, the most spiritual one among us, speculated that Elijah himself may have paid a visit.

As for me, I'll never know the story behind the mysterious paper. Somehow, though, I like to think that my mom was involved, saying that she was beside me. It gives me comfort to think that she played a part in the message from Elijah. I would be facing many challenges and dilemmas in the coming months, and she would be holding my hand as I walked an unknown road. As we counted the stars together, she would guide me on whatever path lay ahead.

Guardian Angels Come
in Many Disguises

Ann Woollcombe

**Some say they're just a human invention . . . yet others believe
that guardian angels watch over us.**

It was getting close to my son-in-law's birthday, and I tried to
find him a Moroccan *tagine*. Chris is an adventurous cook,
and I thought he would appreciate this earthenware pot. (I also
looked forward to the delicious stew that he'd prepare in it.)

When I set out in the morning to go to the Bay, I knew it was
not one of my better days. I'm seventy-something and suffer
from high blood pressure that occasionally goes through the
roof with little or no warning. But though I felt dizzy and a bit
weak, I convinced myself that shopping always had a beneficial
effect on me. So I set out anyway.

The bus dropped me off right at the Rideau Centre, Ottawa's downtown mall, and I made my way up to the cookware department. No *tagines*, but some beautiful stoneware imported from France caught my eye. I went close to get a good look, and then the room began to spin and I fell right into the display—miraculously not breaking a thing. Panic-stricken, I looked around. There was no salesperson in sight. I felt ill and not ready for any confrontation, so I took the elevator, which happened to be nearby, and made it to the first floor.

The elevator door opened onto a dubious-looking thoroughfare that connects Rideau Street with the Byward Market. I made it to a metal bench and looked around me. This corridor is usually frequented by young toughs. Drugs change hands, and the police frequently arrest people here. How was I going to get out? How would I get home?

A gang of several young men sporting Mohawk hairdos, chains, tattoos, and clattering boots came through the back door. I do not know what propelled me to grab one of these boys by the arm. "Please, guys, I need help. I don't feel well, but I would get home all right if you could take me outside and help me get on the Number 18 bus." The boys stopped and looked at me, puzzled. But then their leader took me by the arm, and they all marched me outside and, oh miracle, the Number 18 bus was approaching. "Will you be OK?" they asked, and even told the driver I needed a seat. I reached home, very thankful to see my bed. I am convinced that these scary-looking boys, though in strange disguise, were my guardian angels.

PART SIX
Friendship

A man who has friends must himself be friendly,
But there is a friend who sticks closer than a brother.
    —Proverbs 18:24

Two are better than one,
Because they have a good reward for their labor.
For if they fall, one will lift up his companion.
But woe to him who is alone when he falls,
For he has no one to help him up.
    —Ecclesiastes 4:9–10

This is My commandment, that you love one another as I have loved you.
    —John 15:12

And just as you want men to do to you, you also do to them likewise.
    —Luke 6:31

Be kindly affectionate to one another with brotherly love, in honor giving preference to one another.
    —Romans 12:10

NO FRIENDSHIP IS AN ACCIDENT

A friend is someone who knows all about you and still loves you.
—Elbert Hubbard

Don't walk behind me; I may not lead. Don't walk in front of me;
I may not follow. Just walk beside me and be my friend.
—Albert Camus

I would rather walk with a friend in the dark than alone in the
light.

—Helen Keller

No friendship is an accident.

—O. Henry

We must find time to stop and thank the people who make a difference in our lives.

—John F. Kennedy

Friendship is born at that moment when one person says to
another: "What! You too? I thought I was the only one."

—C.S. Lewis

In prosperity our friends know us; in adversity we know our friends.

—John Churton Collins

You can always tell a real friend: when you've made a fool of yourself he doesn't feel you've done a permanent job.

—Laurence J. Peter

A friend is a gift you give yourself.

—Robert Louis Stevenson

The severest test of character is not so much the ability to keep a secret as it is, when the secret is finally out, to refrain from disclosing that you knew it all along.

— Sydney J. Harris

The best mirror is an old friend.

—George Herbert

The language of friendship is not words but meanings.

—Henry David Thoreau

A Letter to a Friend

Arden and Jean Robertson

Arden and Jean are chapel volunteers for the prisons in Mission, British Columbia. They have been volunteering at several prisons for more than thirty-five years and have been honored by Correctional Service Canada and the National Volunteer Association for their fine and dedicated work. They care greatly for those on the "outside" as well as those on the "inside" of the law. We have worked with them, all of us following this thought, attributed to Robert Pierce: "Let my heart be broken for the things that break God's heart."

Dear Margaret:

Many years ago, we came across the poem "Footprints." As it is for others, at times life is a struggle and we go around carrying a heavy load.

When we first heard this poem, it gave us so much hope, peace, and joy to know that through all the problems of life, the Lord was indeed carrying us through the tough times, as well as the good times.

Because we have been so touched by this poem, we have always appreciated the fact that you and Paul visited the federal prisons to share this poem with the inmates. We know that many of these people are there because of wrong choices in their lives. As they sit in these institutions, there is great heartache and pain. Many have lost all hope in this life as they face lengthy prison sentences.

When the inmates are introduced to this poem, you can see the joy on their faces to know they can go through this journey of incarceration and really understand the Lord is carrying them through the tough times.

Many of these men have asked for a copy of this much-loved poem. A copy of the poem also hangs on the chapel wall.

Thank you so much, Margaret, for sharing this poem with us and the inmates we visit. You have blessed so many people with your gift of poetry, and for that we are grateful.

God bless you,

Arden and Jean Robertson

What Are the Chances?

Cherry Dawn Bolognese

One of the personal blessings of "Footprints" has been the opportunity to meet people and forge friendships. Mostly, we're introduced face to face—at a booksellers' conference, at a bookstore, or in church. A few such meetings have even taken place on a plane. I think one of the most profound encounters happened when a gentleman from Ballarat, Australia, phoned me. He was on a cross-country trip of Canada, and his wife had given him my book *Footprints: The True Story Behind the Poem That Inspired Millions*. He called from Kingston, Ontario, where their bus had broken down (and, coincidentally, where I had penned the poem), and we arranged to meet in Vancouver—on the only day we were available between our church camp engagements. We had a fantastic and memorable day with his family.

So when a woman by the name of Cherry Dawn phoned and wanted to share her story with me, I was unprepared for where that conversation would lead. As you'll see, we had unknowingly been neighbors decades before. To my knowledge, I hadn't met her all those years ago, but I had observed her many times walking her dog past our home, when our children were very young. Several Kleenexes later, I was physically exhausted and spiritually high from the experience of realizing that the poem had woven its way through another person's life like the threads in a weaver's loom.

It started with some bad news involving our home and future planning, made more difficult because my husband had been forced into retirement with five degenerative disks and arthritis in his back. He had also suffered a mild heart attack one year after retirement. Several faith-shaking events had occurred around the same time, and I was feeling quite low—I could not shake the feeling of having let down my husband and children.

My darling husband likes to check out the local thrift store. Around this time he brought home a painting that I had admired, plus a small book by Squire Rushnell, called *When God Winks at You: How God Speaks Directly to You through the Power of Coincidence*. "I think you're going to like this one," my husband said, as he handed me the book. Mr. Rushnell writes that, if you look back to the major crossroads in your life, you start to see coincidences all around them. These coincidences let you know that you are on a path that is right for you.

I read the book and, looking back, did see some signs and coincidences around major life events. One night, not long after I had finished the book, a friend and I were driving into town to go for a coffee. As I was explaining the book to her, I looked over to my right—and pulled the car over in amazement. There, in living color, was the "painting" my husband had brought home: same colors in the sky, full moon through the trees. And though there was no snow in the foreground (because I live in British Columbia), the moonlight had turned the grass silvery white. Wow! What are the chances? So I said to my friend, "That's a wink from God." Then I added, "It's nice to see, but right now I could use a road sign, a map, a navigator . . . something a little more, though I don't know what."

The next morning I drove into town to do some errands. A woman was putting out a box of books—free books—in front of the thrift shop. To a bibliophile like me, it was like discovering a box of no-calorie chocolates. *Oh, Cherry,* I said to myself. *You have so many books. Leave those alone!* Still, I felt I absolutely had to look through the box. I picked up a couple of softcover novels, a history book, and, for my grandson, a book of very bad monster jokes. I was quite satisfied with my finds but, as I turned toward my car, a very quiet voice inside me said, *Look one more time.* So I returned to the box to find a hardcover book sitting right on top.

It was a book by Margaret Fishback Powers, *Footprints: The True Story Behind the Poem That Inspired Millions*.

Now, I know that book hadn't been there thirty seconds earlier. I had thoroughly pawed through the little treasure trove of books. But I have great affection for the poem and thought, *I would like to know where that poem comes from.* So I picked up the book and went home.

Later in the day I curled up with the book, my dog, and a cup of tea. I was so moved by the story of Mr. and Mrs. Powers that I couldn't put the book down. I saw "God winks" in her story—similarities between some of the events in the book and challenging times we had gone through. My heart went out to her when she shared the story of her daughter's fall over the waterfall, and her husband's heart attack. I empathized when the Powers were overworked and found their patience tried. Moreover, I saw how Mr. and Mrs. Powers overcame the hard times with self-realization, love, determination, and great faith in God. Her story helped me to see the bitterness taking root in my own heart. Her faith, expressed in the chapters of the book, helped me to pull that root of bitterness out of my garden.

Mrs. Powers wrote about her life in the Don Mills area of Toronto and the Anglican church on Victoria Park Avenue. When I read about the loss of her poems—a piece of her heart— it struck a chord with me. I too had lost an art. I had been taught to play classical piano, jazz tenor sax, clarinet, and flute. But after a car accident, when I was hit by a drunk driver, I was unable to play for years.

In her book, Mrs. Powers explained how her family had ended up in Coquitlam, British Columbia. I felt moved to phone her and tell her how much her poem had meant to our family. Indeed, I was moved to tell her that, through her art, she had helped countless people get through a tough day or heal a wounded soul. I wanted to give her a hug and to say thank you for writing such an inspirational work. After all this thinking, I told myself, *Well, that's just silly. What are the chances of finding the Powers in Coquitlam? They probably have moved.*

A very quiet voice within me answered, *What harm to look up the number?*

But I phoned directory assistance and did get a number.

What are the chances it's the same Powers family? the voice asked.

But I dialed . . . and it was the right family.

What are the chances the Powers would even talk to me?

Minutes later, I was starting a conversation with Mr. P. We chatted for a while, and I mentioned all the things I wanted to say to Mrs. Powers. He suggested I phone back later and talk to her personally. Then, just before we finished our conversation, I mentioned that I'd lived in Don Mills around the same time his family did. I told Mr. Powers I lived in the vicinity of Highway 401, Don Mills Road, and the Don Valley Parkway. "We lived there, too," Mr. Powers said, "at number 89 Tulane Crescent."

I almost fell off the chair. "For Pete's sake," I replied. "I lived at number 41."

Later that day, I phoned Mrs. Powers. We had a long chat, and she remembered me from all those years ago walking my Dalmatian past her home. Sometimes her daughters would pat my dog. Not only that, but the Powers ministered at the Anglican church I attended when I was young.

Such a small world it is. The stranger who wrote a poem that helped me, and countless others, through hard times and good ones was a neighbor from long ago.

I guess you could call that a wink, a sign, a map, a navigator— or whatever else you wish. No matter. I say thank you to God, who runs this wonderful place.

A Package Deal

Rebecca Nordquist

*With all lowliness and gentleness, with longsuffering, bearing
with one another in love, Endeavoring to keep the unity of the
Spirit in the bond of peace.*
—Ephesians 4:2–3

One of the wisest pieces of advice on friendship I ever received
was from one of my daughters. She's in middle school. You
know, that awkward place where insecurities run rampant, hor-
mones rage, and your best friend one day becomes your worst
enemy the next? So lovely!

One day when I picked her up from school, she got in the car
with tears filling her eyes. She waited until we pulled out of the
parking lot to let all her hurt leak down her cheeks. "Rough day?"
I asked.

"Awful," she replied.

I turned down the radio, waited until we were at a red light, and reached for her hand. "Want to talk about it?"

"Nope," she whispered as she turned her face away from me toward the window. The rest of the night she sulked around the house. And no matter how many times I tried to get her to talk, this normally very vocal child wouldn't open up.

The next morning, I was surprised when she bounded down the stairs with a smile on her face. "Well, hey! You sure look happy this morning," I said as I lifted up quick thank-you prayers to God for whatever had brought back the sunshine to my girl's life.

"Mom," she said with great authority. "I've decided something about friends. They all have good stuff and bad stuff. Things you like and things that really annoy you. So, you just have to decide if you can handle their package deal."

How wise. How true. Friends are a package deal. And sadly, not all friendships will stand the test of time. Some friendships are for a season. But other times, we have to be willing to deal with the messy stuff to fight for our friendships.

Recently, I had something difficult happen with a friend I dearly love and greatly respect—a misunderstanding, hurt feelings, and frustration. Part of me wanted to distance myself because it was hard to sift through the hurt. But as I prayed through it, I had to remind myself this person is a package deal. Part of what makes my friend so great is her tenacity and passion. But because she's so task-oriented, she also has a very sensitive side.

And if I'm honest with myself, I can see that I'm a package deal, too—with good stuff and annoying stuff. My friend has issues, and I have issues. But we're both fully aware we're going to hit some muddy little potholes along our friendship path. But we've decided the package deal is worth it.

Dear Lord, thank You for my friendships. I know some will last a lifetime, and some will fade after a short season. Please help me be completely humble and gentle, patient, bearing with my friends in love.

Life's "Other" Moments

Ray Granet

At times we need just a gentle boost to lift our spirits.

I was reading the inspirational poem "Footprints in the Sand," and wondered how the poet's words applied to my life.

I've been blessed with good health and a wonderful, supportive family. Sure, I've had challenges in my life. But, thank God, I can't say I've had many crises. I have dear friends who have valiantly fought battles against life-threatening diseases, and others who have had turmoil in their personal lives. They have surely experienced the trials and tests described so powerfully in the last lines of the poem.

My neighbor Jacqui, now in her eighties, faced a life-threatening experience a few years ago. Her friends had asked her to join them on a cruise of the North Sea. When the ship docked off the coast of Scotland on a wet day, Jacqui lost her footing as she walked along a slippery wooden plank high above the crashing waves. She reached for a rail, only to discover there was none—and she found herself plunging down into the rocky waters. When she was in her seventies, Jacqui had taken judo lessons—and she credits those lessons with teaching her how to fall and saving her life. She landed on her knees rather than on her head. Still, her injuries were severe, and she found herself in the local hospital of a small seaside town for four long weeks, recovering from several surgeries. One morning a friendly visitor came into her room, carrying flowers and holding a card. She imagined he was there to see her roommate, but no, he was the man who ran the newsstand in the hospital lobby. He had heard about Jacqui's accident, and thought he'd say hello. That afternoon, the man's wife paid Jacqui a visit as well. For the rest of her stay, either the man or his wife or both of them dropped in to spend some time with Jacqui. She firmly believes they not only lifted her spirits, but were God's messengers, who lifted her up, throughout her ordeal.

There have been no such "big moments" in my life. I've had setbacks at work and a couple of health scares. But as I thought about the message of the poem, I realized that messengers don't wait just for huge challenges. They also quietly show up at different points in our lives, when we need a gentle boost. One example comes quickly to mind—the story of the green pen.

I work as an editor, and years ago—in the era before computers—part of my job was to color code a manuscript for the designer. If I marked a paragraph in red, it received one style of treatment: it was my way of telling the designer to put a box around the words. Blue meant something else. And so did green. I was fighting a tight deadline. It was a Sunday morning, and I was having coffee with my new neighbor, Nancy, telling her of my dilemma. I had to deliver my work first thing the next morning, and though my bucket of pens included a large selection of blue, red, and black, there was no green. By chance, did Nancy have a green pen? No, she didn't.

After coffee I went back to work—there was still a lot to do before I began the coding part of the job. At four in the afternoon, I thought I had better take a precious hour or two out of my day to start driving through town, on my hunt for a green pen. Just then, I heard a knock on the door. It was Nancy, and I was about to tell her that I didn't have time for a chat. But before I could say a word, she held out a tiny brown paper bag and asked, "Is this what you need?"

And there it was—the elusive green pen.

That story took place in 1997—more than fifteen years ago. I'm still editing, although color coding is, thankfully, a thing of the past. But on my desk is an old jar, with many of the tools of my trade in it—a few sharp pencils, a red pen, a trusty eraser or two, a small ruler, a bunch of paper clips, and—among all those items— an old green pen that may no longer write, but will always remind me of why Nancy is still such a very special part of my life.

No Matter How Heavy Our Problems

Elizabeth Cranston

Where to begin when it comes to my friend Liz Cranston? She's from Northern Ireland and, with her wonderful husband, Ian, helped host us when we did our exciting and memorable work in that country.

The first time I met Liz, I was speaking in Belfast. When I had finished and returned to our book table, Liz came up to me and asked how I was feeling. I said, "Fine—but why were you wondering?" She then told me she worked in physical therapy and would give me a treatment on my feet. She thought we had been traveling for too long and that (by that time) I was limping a bit and my back was out of place. She was right! After a couple of treatments, I was ready to take the train to Dublin to do some important work and ministry in the schools, and visit the

Footprints in the Sand bookstore. (Discovering that store was one of the biggest surprises of our married life.)

Years after the events of this story, set during difficult times, Queen Elizabeth and the Duke of Edinburgh spent time in Ireland—and wore the green. Their visit gave us a wonderful feeling about the importance of peace and forgiveness.

Coming from a country town in Northern Ireland named Banbridge (where Joseph Scriven, the author of "What a Friend We Have in Jesus," was born), I was brought up in the Presbyterian Church, where my father was an elder. My sister and I went to Sunday school and attended church and our parents encouraged us to join and enjoy the many organizations that held meetings at the church during the week. Later, I taught Sunday school and was a member of the choir. Although involved in these activities, I wasn't actually walking with the Lord (that didn't happen until I was in my forties). But I never once thought I wasn't a Christian, and I believed I would be going to heaven when that time came.

Many years on, I married my husband, Ian, and we had two children: a son, Paul, and a daughter, Anne. We moved to another town to be near Ian's work. I started my own business in natural therapies, the most prominent one being reflexology. We had a great life and things went well for us as a family.

One time while on holiday, our young daughter spotted a framed, illustrated copy of the poem "Footprints in the Sand." She bought it and, when we returned home, put it up on the wall in her bedroom, where it remained for many years. Sometime later my husband redecorated Anne's room, and the poem was put away in a box in the attic. Years later I moved my business to work above a health shop, and Ian decorated my treatment room. I remembered the "Footprints" picture and thought it would be a nice touch to put it on the wall there. It was quite a talking point with my clients. Many times they were able to relate it to situations in their lives, which made it easier for them to talk to me and discuss sensitive matters.

Over the past few months I've been sorting out drawers. I came across a file with letters, cards, and some pictures that the children made during their primary school years. Opening and reading over these papers brought me back to the time when Paul and Anne were youngsters. I found a pink envelope that had a poem typed on a child's typewriter. The title, "Footprints," was underlined in red, and this letter was written in Anne's neat handwriting:

Dear Mum,
I hope you like the Footprints things, I am hungry, I love you so much I could eat you all up. I think the story Footprints is a lovely story it is nice to know that he picks you up when you are in trouble.
Love, Anne—xoxo

It was so nice to find these letters that had been put away for so many years and to know that a child understood the meaning of the poem when she was so young.

The poem's biggest impact on my life came when my husband was very ill in hospital and I was working and looking after our two children. I went in to work on Monday morning (Ian had been taken to hospital the day before) and was with a client. She and I were sitting at the treatment couch when the owner of the health shop came running up the stairs, shouting for us to get out—there was a bomb in the street outside the shop. In his haste to get out of the shop he had forgotten about us in the room above. But suddenly he remembered and came tearing back, shouting, "There's a bomb outside! Get out now!" My client and I raced out to the street, just moments before the bomb went off. The next day we were allowed into the shop. It was a total mess, and my room was wrecked. The treatment couch where we had been sitting was ripped apart and covered in shards of glass from the two large windows. We probably wouldn't have survived—or if we had, we would have been very badly cut and scarred. All the furniture was smashed and things in the room were blown everywhere. Yet the picture on the wall with the "Footprints in the Sand" poem was intact. In the weeks that followed, the Lord truly carried me. Ian was in hospital, my workplace was gone. I was lost.

A few years back I was privileged to meet Margaret and Paul

Powers and have them in our home. They were in Ireland to speak about their lives. Hearing Margaret talk about the story behind the poem was a memorable experience. We all have times in our lives when we don't realize we have been carried by the Lord, and we wonder, when we look back, just how we got through this or that situation. Things go well and then, all of a sudden, we feel as if someone has pulled a rug from under our feet and we are tumbling in midair and can't get our feet back on the ground. That's when the Lord comes and carries us. I know this has happened to me many, many times in my life. I may not have always known the Lord was there, but now I am so thankful that He was and realize what He has done for me.

In my work I have been able to use the poem to explain and help people understand that instead of being left on our own, we have the Lord with us. No matter how heavy our problems weigh, He will carry us when we are in trouble.

The Diploma

Susie Morgan

Kindness shines through and, years later, still lifts our spirits.

Even thirty years after we graduated from high school, Eleanor is still Ellie to me. Throughout my high school years in New York City, Ellie and I had adventures. We both loved the theater, and after school, on a matinee day, we'd sneak in at intermission to see a show—well, half a show. I can't tell you how many second acts we saw! We both loved chocolate cake, and often before school, we'd meet in the park and share something delicious that one of us had picked up at the bakery. We also loved meeting celebrities and used to hang out in the lobbies of the swank hotels in the city, hoping for a sighting.

Ellie was more popular than I was—far more popular. But we had a special bond. We laughed at the same things. And even though classmates thought I was unconventional while Ellie seemed the height of respectability, we both loved to write, we both felt we should have been born in an earlier time, and—I hope I don't sound boastful—we were both basically kind kids who liked to make strangers smile.

As for our differences, there were many. Most notably, my home life was unhappy, while Ellie's family was traditional and support-ive. My dad was cold and distant, and my mom was highly critical. She also suffered from a disorder that often made her withdrawn. There was no dinnertime conversation in our home, no games after dinner, no family picnics—all things that Ellie took for granted. That's why I loved visiting her home, where I was welcomed as part of the family. The rare time Ellie visited me, I worried about my mom's erratic behavior. She tended to say inappropriate and embarrassing things, but Ellie took it all in her stride.

In high school I took our friendship for granted, but only after we graduated did I come to appreciate the great difference she had made in my life. I think the event that best sums up her kindness was our graduation ceremony.

Our art teacher, Miss Kelley, an eccentric but kind person, had hand-lettered each of our diplomas. Her script was exquisite, with beautiful flourishes, and I cherished the piece of paper that said that I, Susie Harris, had completed my high school years.

Both my parents were at the late afternoon ceremony, and after-wards I showed them the diploma with great pride—hoping for, but really not expecting, the warm "Congratulations!" that my classmates were hearing from their parents. What I heard, how-ever, shattered all the happiness of the day. My dad took one look at the diploma and lashed out at me. "Susie? Susie? Why does your diploma say Susie? You are *Susan*. That's what it should say, and don't come home until it does!"

I knew my schoolmates could hear my father, and I was crushed, frightened, and humiliated. I tried to hold in my sobs, and as I walked away, Ellie came over to me, put her arm around me, and said I should tell my parents that I'd be spending the night at her home.

I wanted to disappear, but she convinced me to join her family for a graduation dinner at a French restaurant. I didn't have much of an appetite, but I pretended to enjoy my meal because I didn't want to appear downbeat.

The next morning at school, I went to the art room and asked Miss Kelley a favor—could she please, please fix my diploma? She did so graciously, and I think the new version had even fancier flourishes than the old one.

Ellie and I went our separate ways after high school. She went to an out-of-state college and I took a job before returning to school years later. About five years ago we tracked each other down and, although we now live on opposite coasts, we talk regularly. Not long ago I reminded her about our graduation. She said she barely remembered the diploma incident. I told her that I would never forget how her innate kindness shone through on that night.

Today, I'm the very proud mom of a son who is soon to graduate from high school. I can't wait to hug him after he receives his diploma. I like to think that I brought him up with all the love and understanding that I missed out on in my own childhood. And if I've done my job, then I think it's because I hung around with Ellie.

Reconnecting

Jean Anderson

Reminiscing, sharing a laugh, and counting blessings—finding an old friend is a wonderful gift.

I first remember seeing the "Footprints" poem in the late 1970s. It had a huge impact on my life, especially between the end of 1979 and 1981. I was going through a very difficult time in our marriage, and the words of "Footprints" ministered to me many times over. Through the words of the poem, God spoke to me to remind me that He never left me, even when I felt so alone. The good news is that our marriage was restored. We are about to celebrate our fortieth wedding anniversary.

Since that time, I have given the poem to many of my friends when they were walking through their own valleys of doubt and difficulty. One of these people was a special teacher with whom

I kept in touch over the years, sharing my faith. She was greatly ministered to by it.

This poem has yet another special meaning for me. When I first read it, I did think the author was "unknown." However, years later I was to find out to my utter surprise that it was someone I had known back in the late 1950s, when we worked together at a church camp in Ontario.

It is so strange but, though I had forgotten most of the staff I worked with back then, I could not get Margaret out of my mind. Often when she came to my thoughts, I felt the compelling need to pray for her. I knew where she had been raised and, every time I heard her town mentioned, would again think of her and pray for her. Little did I realize until I read her story about "Footprints" just how much she had been going through. Her major trials occurred during the period when I was praying a lot for her. God is faithful to guide us in praying for others.

Margaret and I have a lot in common. She went on to become a missionary teacher. I also was a teacher. Writing poetry is something else we have in common.

It was my happy privilege, after nearly forty-seven years, to finally reconnect with Margaret and to meet her wonderful husband, Paul. Since my husband, John, and I moved to British Columbia to work with a Light to the World Ministries (a mission to Haiti), we have had some wonderful times together reminiscing and laughing about the old days and sharing stories of God's faithfulness to both our families.

"Footprints" will continue to be one of my favorite poems, and I am sure it will continue to minister to me in times when I need to be lifted up.

Shrek, and a Beautiful Friendship

Lázaro da Silva Pinto

While in São Paulo, Brazil, with the Portuguese publishers of *Footprints: The True Story Behind the Poem That Inspired Millions*, we were often warned about our safety and security. As a result, we felt almost confined to our hotel. However, one day, the manager arranged for us to go to a nearby luxury mall. As we arrived in the wide, elegant entrance area, we saw what looked like silver telephone booths, but discovered they were portholes with guns poking out of them. As you'll read, that visit to the mall turned out to hold a magical surprise for us.

My name is Lázaro. I live in the town of Santo André, just outside São Paulo, a city of about 15 million people in southern Brazil. I'm a university professor and computer engineer. My wife, Sonia, is a retired physical education teacher. We have two daughters. Livia is a logician, and Melina an endocrinologist.

On a cool afternoon in late June 2003, my wife asked me to go with her to the Higienópolis Mall in São Paulo. Our daughter Melina was with us. I don't like to go shopping, but when I do go, I prefer to visit bookstores and sporting goods stores.

While my wife and Melina went shopping, I found myself walking through the mall concourse. As I passed an electronics store, I observed a salesman struggling to communicate with an elegant-looking couple. Curious, I heard the couple speak English—but the poor salesman didn't understand a word. Brazil is a Portuguese-speaking country (our neighbors in South America speak Spanish). Since my English is passable—at the intermediate level—I thought I'd offer to help. It turned out the couple were interested not in anything involving electronics, but in a large poster of the movie *Shrek*, which was part of a display in the window. I introduced myself and soon learned they were Canadian missionaries, and that the woman was a writer of inspirational Christian books. My daughter is fluent in English, so I called on her to meet the couple—Paul and Margaret Powers.

Our family is evangelical, and we were delighted to meet this couple who had come so far to visit our country. We asked Margaret about her books and she told us she was the author of the very moving poem "Footprints" and had come to Brazil to promote the Brazilian Portuguese release of her book *Footprints: The True Story Behind the Poem that Inspired Millions.*

We had all heard about this very powerful, moving poem,

and now we were thrilled. We believe in God and the wonders of His work, and truly He had placed me in front of two very special people.

Paul and Margaret told us they had been in São Paulo for three days but did not know our city. Nobody from the publishing office had been able to arrange a tour, and they had been warned not to walk alone, since it could be very dangerous. But I couldn't let them leave our magnificent city without seeing it, and I wanted them to have a good impression of where we lived. Paul told me a journalist would be accompanying them on several engagements throughout the city. He suggested that I speak to her and arrange for a day when they could tour the city with us.

The next day I spoke to the journalist, who—for safety reasons—checked to confirm who I was. She gave her approval, and I called Paul and Margaret to make arrangements to pick them up at their hotel the following day.

The tour took us to the art museum; Paulista Avenue—said to be the trendiest avenue in Latin America; Morumbi Stadium, which hosts major soccer games—the passion of Brazilians; and our beautiful Ibirapuera Park (reminiscent of New York City's Central Park). The evening ended with dinner at an Italian restaurant called Familia Mancini, where Paul admired an eighty-pound piece of cheese. Making the day even more perfect was the fact that Paul and Margaret were celebrating their thirty-fifth wedding anniversary. Fantastic!

We met two more times and went to a service at the Presbyterian church, where Margaret shared the story of how and why she wrote "Footprints." Paul spoke about his life-changing experiences, and also told us about the walk on the beach that inspired Margaret to write her poem. The congregants were deeply moved and honored to have the Canadian guests visit them. Our young pastor translated their stories.

After the service, we returned to our apartment and had Brazilian pizza. Before they returned to Canada, the Powers invited us to their hotel for farewell coffee. We sealed our friendship! Paul told me how grateful he was for our hospitality, and I said that Brazilians are like that, especially when we find "brothers of the faith."

For two years we exchanged emails, postcards, and photos. Margaret and Paul continued to invite us to visit their home, their church, and Vancouver—their beautiful and famous city. It's not easy to plan international trips but, with the grace of God, we were able to visit Paul and Margaret in 2005. They greeted us at the Vancouver airport. It was easy to spot them—Margaret was wearing the yellow shirt of the Brazilian national soccer team that we had sent her.

I always tell my Brazilian friends I know the city of Vancouver and Vancouver Island better than any other visitor. When we arrived at the Powers' home, Paul and Margaret took me to

Paul's home office and showed me a file folder titled "Lázaro's schedule." They took us to so many beautiful places in Vancouver—including their church—and we were even introduced to the mayor. Other destinations included the famous Harrison Hot Springs, plus three days on Vancouver Island, where we met "Grandma Lucie," who was especially delighted to chat with our daughter, who was soon to become a medical doctor in Brazil. The two of them went hand-in-hand everywhere, and our daughter promised to return to visit again someday.

Margaret and Paul are gifts that God has given our family. They demonstrate their step-by-step action of faith and encouragement, inspiring others to follow in the footprints of the Lord. Now they are part of our family, and their names are always remembered whenever we get together in our home. We ask the good Lord to protect them from all evil, and to give them health and joy to be able to deliver God's Word through poetry, through books such as this one, and by speaking to all who need to hear what they say.

PART SEVEN
Gratitude

Let your conduct be without covetousness; be content with such things as you have. For He Himself has said, "I will never leave you nor forsake you."
—Hebrews 13:5

You will show me the path of your life;
In Your presence is fullness of Joy;
At Your right hand are pleasures forevermore.
—Psalm 16:11

These things I have spoken to you, that My joy may remain in you, and that your joy may be full.
—John 15:11

My brethren, count it all joy when you fall into various trials, knowing that the testing of your faith produces patience.
—James 1:2–3

Thanks be to God for His indescribable gift!
—2 Corinthians 9:15

JOY IS NOT IN THINGS

Don't cry because it's over. Smile because it happened.

—Dr. Seuss

Feeling gratitude and not expressing it is like wrapping a present and not giving it.

—William Arthur Ward

The highest tribute to the dead is not grief but gratitude.

—Thornton Wilder

Let us be grateful to people who make us happy; they are the charming gardeners who make our souls blossom.

—Marcel Proust

The longer I live, the more beautiful life becomes.

—Frank Lloyd Wright

A smile goes a long way, but you must start it on its journey.

—Helen Keller

A good laugh is sunshine in the house.

—William Makepeace Thackeray

You can't change the past, but you can ruin the present by worrying about the future.

—Isak Dinesen

Grief can take care of itself, but to get the full value of a joy you must have somebody to divide it with.

—Mark Twain

Joy is not in things; it is in us.

—Richard Wagner

A good laugh heals a lot of hurts.

—Madeleine L'Engle

If you haven't any wrinkles, you haven't laughed enough.

—Phyllis Diller

There is no beautifier of complexion, or form, or behavior, like the wish to scatter joy and not pain around us.

—Ralph Waldo Emerson

I've learned that people will forget what you said, people will forget what you did, but people will never forget how you made them feel.

—Maya Angelou

A Blessing in My Life

Carlos Cepeda

This very special letter is from Carlos, a young pastor and missionary. Carlos left Cuba on his own, without his wife and family, to be a missionary in St. Vincent and the Grenadines in the West Indies. He had to learn a new language and deal with a completely different culture. His family and church were finally able to raise funds for Carlos's wife, Zenia, and their children to join him. Carlos and Zenia now minister in a remote area. The area of St. Vincent (in the north) where he now lives—Biabou—is beautiful, but extremely rugged. Carlos is a talented musician and fine artist—but most important, he is a fine human being.

Dear Paul and Margaret,

What a great blessing that you are in my life. Even before I met you, I was deeply blessed through you. I feel that God orchestrated our lives a long time ago. Now, when I stop to hear His majestic symphony, I wonder why we don't take more time to appreciate God's music and allow Him to carry us in His arms.

I have a lot to be thankful for. This year, God opened a new ministry for us, with even greater challenges and difficulties, but with the joy to serve. Your poem "Footprints" has been a blessing in my life. It is a privilege to tell you how it has enriched my life.

My first encounter with "Footprints" was in the early 1990s, when I was a teenager studying art. At the time, I was a recent convert. One of my teachers created a beautiful painting that illustrated the poem. What attracted me to it most were the blue tones of the sea, and the figure of a man in the distance, walking toward the sunshine. The words of the poem appeared on the right-hand side of the painting.

Over the years, I have heard the poem many times—it is very well known in Cuba. I even tried to illustrate the poem in 2001, the year I began my journey with the Lord. I had recently graduated and was engaged to a wonderful woman. It was a great blessing to feel the calling of my missions. Everything was going well until one day my doctor discovered I suffered from congenital heart disease. I was told it would affect the quality of my life. For a moment, I felt that my dreams had all been put on hold.

My mom was in the corner of the room, tears in her eyes, and my dad stayed quiet. There was nothing to be done—only medicine, which hopefully would keep my heart beating at a normal rate. My thoughts were somewhere else. In my soul, I grieved, hopeless. What future was there for me, for my bride, for my calling? Looking for an answer, I turned to my Bible, and in the pages I found the poem "Footprints." Suddenly, it was clear to me and I felt at peace. I was not alone. I was not forgotten. I was not abandoned. I asked the Lord if he would take me in His arms, and He heard me.

Eleven years later, I am blessed with a wonderful wife and children, and grateful to be doing God's work. I have faced difficulties during this time—but always I remember that the Lord is with me, carrying me when I need Him most. As this pilgrim continues on his journey through life, "Footprints" reminds me that God will never forsake me.

May God continue to bless you and your family,
Carlos

The Silver Lining

Nancy Perrin

Even years later, an old kindness reminds us that dark clouds do have a silver edge, and that a setback can be reversed by a guardian angel.

Many of my friends avoid going to the dentist. They procrastinate, they cancel, or they arrive in a bad mood. Not me! A remarkable young dental surgeon and his colleague changed the course of my life when everything else was crumbling around me. Now that I reflect on that time, fifty years ago, I realize they gave me my smile. More than that, they instilled in me the belief that something higher and more powerful is at work in my life.

Face it. There is nothing more important to a fourteen-year-old girl than her appearance. It was obvious that my jaw was jutting out and crooked, and to make things worse, I had just arrived in the big city of Toronto from small-town Ontario, population three hundred. It was a typical small town of the late 1950s: skating on the creek with a shy boy who offers to tie your skates; hardtop convertibles, and Jerry Lee Lewis records; doors you never lock; and telephone party lines buzzing with gossip, much of it cruel. Unfortunately, my family was the subject of some of the town's whispers. My father had just lost his business, and suddenly we were broke. Adding to the humiliation was the stigma of finding all our possessions being auctioned off on the sidewalk. My twin sisters and I were heartbroken to be moving away from our childhood friends and scared of the idea of starting over in a big, unfriendly new city.

Shortly after we arrived in Toronto, my mom took me to a much-needed appointment with the neighborhood dentist—a handsome, self-confident, fresh-faced young man, just two years into his practice. Although Dr. Alan Green's office was near our home, it was on the right side of the tracks—so it could have been a hundred miles away. Caring and kind, he took an immediate interest in an attention-starved girl and invited my parents to a meeting, where he advised them that there might be a solution to my condition, which he explained was called "prognathism"—a protruding jaw with an extended chin. Dr. Green was being mentored by one of the top oral surgeons in the country, Dr. Albert Antoni. It seemed this remarkable surgeon performed surgery so expertly that his students didn't see his hands move. If my parents would be willing, Dr. Green would arrange for my surgery.

Thankfully, my parents agreed to the operation. I later learned that, at the same time, Dr. Green had another patient, my age, with the same condition. Her parents would not allow her jaw to be touched because they believed that God wanted her to be that way.

What I remember most about that time is missing school for a couple of weeks. I spent a full week in the hospital, my face swollen beyond recognition—intravenous tubes connected to my arm. My mom visited me every day after she finished work. I also remember that my jaw was clamped tight for months afterwards. My family later joked that they enjoyed the quiet.

A few months following the successful completion of the surgery, I passed Dr. Green on the street and said hello. He didn't respond immediately. My jaw and chin and smile had changed so dramatically that he hadn't recognized me.

I have now been a patient of Dr. Green's for fifty years. In all that time, not once has he asked for thanks or any kind of acknowledgment of how he was responsible for altering my appearance and likely changing my future. I believe kindness is simply in the DNA of this modest man and outstanding dentist. I hope he now understands the depth of my gratitude. I was an impressionable kid whose life's direction could have easily taken a different path.

So now, half a century later, I say thank you to the young dentist who, fresh out of school, reached out and gave me a new start. I also thank the late Dr. Antoni.

As a postscript, when I decided to write this essay, I visited Toronto's renowned Faculty of Dentistry to learn more about Dr. Antoni. His portrait is one of four that greet you as you enter the hallowed halls of the esteemed school. I also belatedly asked Dr. Green who had paid for the expensive surgery, which obviously my parents could never have afforded. He suggested that Dr. Antoni had performed it pro bono—out of kindness and compassion. I say thank you to these two remarkable professionals.

Then I asked another question, this one to myself. Would such an opportunity have ever taken place had we stayed in small-town Ontario? Immediately I knew the answer—not a chance!

And a Little Kid Shall Lead Them

Joseph Liebman

"At last I saw what I had always assumed was a figure of speech: the light at the end of the tunnel."

The guidebook said it very clearly: "If you want this walk to be authentic, use a candle. King Solomon did not own a flashlight." The guidebook went on to say that the king had built the tunnel to bring water to Jerusalem and that, nearly three thousand years later, it still did. "Bedouins use it to water their flocks." I turned to the front of the guidebook to locate a map. As I was to find out later, I should have turned to the back.

Jerusalem in April can be a little brisk. Although it is officially springtime, the city is so high up that the actual spring doesn't arrive until June. Ironically—and this is just one of the many ironies of the place—it overlooks the lowest spot on the planet, the Dead Sea. In fact, this is the reason why Solomon had to build his tunnel. The only sources of freshwater are the springs outside the city. And the only way to bring it in is by tunneling through the rocky foundation.

It wasn't easy to find the entrance to the tunnel. The map was clear enough, but not the landscape. A lot of boulders and a great many bushes (none burning). Also, there were no signs. When I did find the entrance, it was not much larger than I was. Fortunately, this was in the 1980s—when I was a lot less large than I am now. I stepped over a boulder and into the gap. And in that moment, the world disappeared.

Remember the ten plagues? This was the ninth, the plague of darkness. The Bible describes it as "a darkness which may be felt." I couldn't describe it better. Whatever daylight might have seeped in from the entrance had been swallowed up by the cave. So I lit the candle, tucked the matchbook under my belt, and held my breath. The only sound I could hear was the water rushing around my feet. I congratulated myself on having worn sandals instead of my heavy hiking boots.

Even with the candle, I could hardly see an inch in front of me. Not that there was much to see. Walls of rock, tufts of moss, and the occasional stalagmite. Or was it a stalactite? I can never remember which. Pale as it was, the candlelight was comforting, and I began to imagine that King Solomon's miners were marching by my side. For a moment I thought that I had actually seen one, but it was only my shadow cast upon the walls.

The guidebook had said it was a fifteen-minute walk to the other end of the tunnel. I hadn't brought a watch with me—not because King Solomon didn't own one, but because I didn't. Even so, I had a pretty good idea what fifteen minutes felt like. After a while, it felt more like thirty. I plodded on. And then, the rocks around me turned a corner, and there it was: a fork in the tunnel. As I recalled, there was nothing in the guidebook about two different streams, at least not as far as I had read. But I wasn't about to panic. That would come later.

When I look back at it all, I still wonder why, at this point, I just didn't turn back. Instead, I decided to take the fork to the left, based largely on no particular reason. Another afterthought: If I had gone to the right, would I have also found myself up to my knees in water? Probably, yes. The guidebook did suggest not taking this walk in early spring. The runoff from the winter rains would make it quite deep, as I would read that night at the hostel where I finished the book.

So there I was, up to my waist in water and not a clue as to how far into the future the exit would be. Did I mention that the candle had gone out? I reached for the matchbook, and realized that it was as soaked as I was. *Now* you can cue to the panic music.

As if I weren't wet enough, I was now dripping with perspiration. Somehow I knew that going forward to an unknown exit in a deepening stream was not going to get me out of here. The one thing I was sure of was that there was an entrance behind me unless, of course, this really was a nightmare. So I swam around and headed back.

It seemed like hours till I came again to the fork in the stream (now a river). It occurred to me that I had no idea which fork I had come from. I might have even come to another fork entirely. It all looked quite different, at least in my mind. In my eyes I could see nothing but the darkness of Egypt. Maybe I could feel my way out.

They say that when one is deprived of one sense, the others are heightened. They also say that one can smell fear, but that isn't the sense I'm talking about. After sloshing around without moving a foot (except for the one that my sandal slipped off), I decided to stop and stand perfectly still. So still that I could hear my heart beating. And a goat bleating.

At first, I couldn't believe my ears. It was so faint that I thought I had imagined it, kind of an acoustic mirage. But after a few seconds I heard it again. So I followed the bleat as well as my heart, and as one grew stronger the other calmed down. At last I saw what I had always assumed was a figure of speech: the light at the end of the tunnel.

I must have looked like the wreck of Hesperus. But the Bedouin boy standing at the entrance didn't seem to care. And neither did his goat. The boy smiled knowingly, as though he had seen this all before. The goat was too busy drinking to even notice I was there. She was just happy that there was so much water. Obviously, she had read the guidebook to the end.

There Was a Plan

Shirley May

For I know the thoughts that I think toward you, says the Lord, thoughts of peace and not of evil, to give you a future and a hope.
—Jeremiah 29:11

My life has not taken a typical route. I grew up on the beautiful East Coast of Canada with my mom, dad, and three siblings. My dad, an American residing in Canada, had a job that moved our family every three years. This prevented me from establishing deep roots in my life. Dad also had a temper and was abusive. Not long after our third move, when I was almost nine years old, we lost Mom to breast cancer. Four years later, Dad married a woman twenty years his junior, and they had two children together. After high school, I left home to attend college on the West Coast. It became evident that I had no place to call "home" when Dad informed me that his new family was his family now. I had lost Mom's nurturing love and lacked the protective hand of a father. I was a naive teenager faced with learning life on my own.

Life by myself meant a lot of bouncing around and a great deal of aloneness. Other students had parents who visited them on campus, sent care packages, and attended graduation. Mother's Day and Father's Day were awkward for me. Holidays such as Thanksgiving and Christmas were filled with conversations about family get-togethers—but none of that related to my life.

About that time, I came across the poem "Footprints in the Sand." I quietly read the poem, allowing each word to slowly penetrate my heart. The poem was a great reminder that God was always with me and I was never alone, no matter how displaced I felt. God hears the cries of our heart and He carries us when we are weary. The poem brought comfort to my quietly sad heart.

After earning my college degree and working at substandard jobs, I secured a sought-after position. For the first time in my life, I had some stability. By now, people my age were married and starting a family. I launched myself into my career, and the years flew past. I did well and earned several promotions. Although I knew God loved me, I often thought that perhaps He had forgotten me. True, He had provided for me well. I was living in a free country, my health was good, and I had a great job. I was content in Him, but I was not content with myself. I was weary of being alone and I longed for someone special who would love me unconditionally.

After ten years of working in a secure job, I could not ignore the restlessness stirring within my heart. I had many dreams, yet I was not pursuing them. With no family around me, my career had become my life. I realized that if I did not make a drastic change, I would grow old full of regrets. An interesting documentary on an employer in New York City caught my attention. I contacted the employer and after conversing and sharing my resume, I was told I had an open invitation to a position in the organization. Living in New York would mean busy surroundings and abundant distractions. And, after the events of September 11, 2001, the city held a special place in my heart. I liked the idea of moving there. However, it is an expensive place to live and because I was alone (or so I thought), I took steps to ensure financial security. I devised a financial plan and followed it diligently for two years. To my dismay, a few months before my planned move, the gentleman who had offered me a position transferred to another organization. The individual who replaced him informed me there were no job openings and recommended not living in New York. A wise Christian man once told me that God opens and closes doors. New York was a "closed door." For two years I had planned this course. Now what? I had money in the bank and no plan.

It suddenly dawned on me that because the US border was

nearby, I could live in the United States and commute to my job in Canada. It would be the first step in changing the course of my life. Using the funds that I had saved for New York City, I purchased a home in the United States a few miles from the Canadian border. I moved to a quaint and very traditional town, where being a single gal in her forties without children was considered "odd," as one senior citizen told me. It was a regular occurrence throughout my life for folks to interrogate me on why I was "still single."

After a few years of commuting to Canada, I tired of the daily bumper-to-bumper traffic. It made for long days and little free time. As timing would have it, my employer offered a buyout to employees and I decided to accept it and pursue employment in my local town. This decision greatly improved my quality of life. I became involved in the community. I found a church to attend and volunteered at the local museum. Within a year, my networking was successful and it landed me a new career with an excellent boss. For the first time in my life, I felt a sense of belonging where I lived.

Then one day, my boss informed me that he had accepted a job offer in another state. I suddenly found myself in limbo again. Even though I loved my job, my boss contributed a great deal to the enjoyable work environment. I was left running the office by myself and, during that time, I began to think of moving back to the East Coast. By now I had concluded that my special someone was not in my current town and I resigned myself to the idea that I might be alone for the rest of my life. This time, I considered moving to Florida. I figured that if I was going to be alone, I would at least enjoy life in warm weather and be near a beach. However, my plan was apparently not God's plan.

Many times over the years, I had prayed for a special man to come into my life. This time was different. Wisdom taught me to pray a longer and more sincere prayer, sharing my heart with God. I (finally) gave my romantic future over to Him to figure out for me. I then proceeded to browse jobs in Florida. I was a homeowner, however, which meant I could not move to another state quickly. I needed a plan.

I was in the early stages of my new plan when, out of nowhere, I received an email from a gal who worked at the museum where I volunteered. She suggested that I meet her single brother. She thought he and I would complement each other. With many unfulfilling courtships in my past, underlying complacency was evident in my mind. Nonetheless, I agreed to meet him. Because I had given it all over to God, I had nothing to lose.

I knew in an instant this man was not just another date. He was kind, humble, and manly, and he loved God. He was everything I wanted in a man. Finally, I had met the man who was made for me. It felt surreal. After years of God carrying me, I landed on my feet to display two sets of footprints in the sand. God said to me, "I have given you a gift." This man is indeed a gift! Unbeknownst to me at the time, God had said to him, "I sent you to her." God had been shaping our lives and preparing us for each other so that we were ready to meet in His perfect time, not our time.

Looking over my life path, it is evident that the grace of God had been carrying me through the years of displacement. God was the lone pair of footprints carrying me to my destination. It boggles my mind when I think of all the maneuvering it took to get me here. Life will not always be perfect. However, God has a perfect plan for you and it is a plan with *your* name written on it. You may not know what you are doing, but God knows what He is doing. Give control of your life to Him and you will discover His awesome plan for you. "For I know the thoughts that I think toward you, says the Lord, thoughts of peace and not of evil, to give you a future and a hope" (Jeremiah 29:11).

Angus's Story

Gus Le Chat (told to a friend)

Struggling to find something that's missing in our life, we ask if it will always elude us. Then we discover the power of prayer.

CALL ME GUS

I'm Angus, but you can call me Gus. I think Angus is too fancy a name for a cat—especially one like me. But someone at the farmhouse decided I looked like an Angus. And the name stuck.

I understand that my mom showed up at the farmhouse one day and just stayed there. There was a warm shed, lots of food in the compost heap, and the occasional mouse. It wasn't a real farm—an older couple from the city lived there, and they traveled back and forth. There were a lot of visitors—and plenty of good food and good smells. There was a dog named Sandy, who would become my pal. But I'm jumping ahead of things. I hadn't even made an appearance. It was just my mom at the time, and she pretty much looked after herself. Then, one day, the couple in the house noticed she was getting bigger. A few weeks later, my brother and I arrived.

Mom looked after us well. She found a warm spot for us in the shed. She'd disappear for a few hours and then return with a treat. After my brother and I got a little bigger, the three of us would walk across the front porch and then stretch out in the sunshine. It was pretty warm, and we'd see the people in the house watch us as we paraded by.

A DECISION

NOT LONG AFTERWARD, something terrible happened. I don't like to think about it, but it is part of my story so I'll tell you what it was. A big animal called a coyote surprised us one night when we came out of the shed. My mom tried to tackle him—but my brother didn't make it. Mom and I put up the fight of our lives, and the coyote finally took off. I still have a scar on my neck.

It was at that time I decided I needed a real home. Some cats are farm cats, but I figured out I was a house cat. What can I say? I knew from the start that I liked people and proper food. (The occasional mouse is fine, but trust me, the scraps of roast beef we found on the porch were so much better.) And the furniture inside the house looked cozy and comfortable. I like the idea of being pampered, and I think I was born to be a pet. I'm a fun guy.

So I began my strategy. I would make myself irresistible. When somebody opened the front door, I'd press my nose against the screen. The old couple tried to ignore me, but I could see them watching what I was up to. Folks thought I was "adorable"—the way I wanted to get inside while Sandy, the dog, tried to get outside. I decided to play the cute card. It was all part of The Plan.

THE PLAN

ONE DAY I HEARD the man explain why they wouldn't bring me inside. There were a few reasons. Every so often, the couple left the house. I think they went to the city. From what I understood, they didn't like the city too much, but sometimes needed to go there. They also went on trips. And once I heard the man tell a visitor that his wife was allergic to cats. I'm not sure what that meant. She liked me, so how could she be allergic?

I also heard the couple say that were getting a little worried about me. The weather was sunny, but the days were growing shorter. The couple didn't like the idea of me being on my own when the cold weather started. Again, I had no idea what that meant. They started to talk about something called winter.

A lot of people were in the house on a weekend in early September. I've always liked people—we were made for each other. A nice woman named Christine fell in love with me. I know that doesn't sound modest, but that's what happened. She was the first of several people who I thought would adopt me. She and her husband had a baby—we were both little creatures. But, as it turned out, I didn't wind up with Christine. We were both disappointed. The story was that she had two other cats, and she didn't think they'd like me. That was the first almost-adoption. There would be more. I was beginning to think that *almost* meant "never." I know that Christine was disappointed—but she had a home and a family. That's all I wanted, too.

One week a woman named Sue came to visit for a few days. Sue also fell in love with me—I heard her say that. And one morning she said that I looked like an "Angus." That's how I got my unusual name. Sue and the couple went for a walk along the road, and I decided to join them. It was hard keeping up with their pace but, at one point, she turned around and saw me racing to keep up with them. They couldn't get over it, and Sue announced that maybe she'd adopt me. Was my plan working?

No, Sue couldn't adopt me either. I'm not sure why, but I'm sure she had reasons. But she said she'd try to find me a home. She would ask her "bridge friends." She would ask her son. But nobody seemed to want a friendly kitten named Angus.

I was starting to get big and, from what I heard, I wouldn't be a kitten for much longer. The food the couple gave me was delicious. These people knew how to eat well. Meanwhile, I was seeing less and less of my mom. We'd sometimes meet at the porch, but she disappeared a lot and seemed perfectly happy to be a farm cat. Not me! I was getting worried about this thing they called winter, and I also knew I would be losing some of the cute factor.

A few days later, I had my first ride in a car. The man put me in a little box, and we drove to a place called the "vet's." What a thrill going for my first drive.

The vet was a nice man. He looked me over—I mean *all* over. He said I had something called ear mites and gave me some drops. He also said that I was too young to be neutered. I had no idea what that meant, but something told me it wasn't a game. Then the vet played with me and said something very interesting. He told the man it's a "scientific fact" that some cats are born with a "social gene." These cats are very special creatures—very playful and very kind. He said that I was born with that gene. Thanks, doctor. I could have told you that—I knew I was social. But I was getting more and more depressed about not being adopted.

A THANKSGIVING PRAYER

It was a holiday called Thanksgiving. I wanted to have something to be thankful for—but it was a time of trouble for me. After six weeks of trying to find a home, I was desperate.

The smells in the house were wonderful. The man and woman gave me some delicious treats called giblets. Then people started to arrive—lots of people. It was a sunny day and the screen door was open. I wanted to lie on my back and enjoy the sunshine, but I was too busy trying to figure out what to do.

The table inside the house looked beautiful. One by one the people sat down. Then everyone was asked to say a Thanksgiving prayer. I didn't know what that meant, but when the people made their prayers I looked at their faces—each face . . . There was something very peaceful, and very powerful, about a prayer. So I said one, too. Nobody ever taught me how to say a prayer, but I knew just how to do it.

Soon they began to eat. The sun was so warm, and I stretched out. Everyone began to notice me, and the couple told the people about how hard they were trying to find me a home.

There was a young woman at the table. Her name was Jami, and I could tell she liked me. She was next to a young man, and from what I overheard, they had just been married. The young woman kept looking at me and smiling, and I smiled right back at her. Then she looked at the young man. "Jimmy," she asked him. "What do you think about adopting Angus?"

I closed my little eyes and said my prayer over and over again. I believed this was my last real chance. How could I let them know how much I wanted a home? Winter was getting closer, I was getting bigger, and things were getting more desperate. So I closed my eyes and prayed, over and over again, that Jimmy and Jami would take me.

Jimmy and Jami weren't sure what to do. They were just start-ing out in life, they both had jobs, and they were thinking about starting a family. Jimmy would say, "Okay," and Jami would say, "Maybe it's not a good idea." Then Jami would say, "But he's so sweet," and Jimmy would ask, "Do we really have the time?" I prayed harder and harder . . . and then Jami said something that made my little ears perk right up.

"Jimmy, let Angus make the decision. When we leave the house, we'll see if he wants to be our cat. If he follows us, then we'll adopt him. If not, he'll have to find another home."

It was now up to me.

About an hour later, Jimmy and Jami gave the man and the woman a big hug and started to walk down the path to their car. Halfway along the laneway, Jami turned her head around. And there I was, happy as could be, scampering quickly in back of them and catching her eye. Then I stopped and turned back for a moment. I saw the house I was leaving, the shed where I was born, and, right behind me in the damp ground, the paw prints that I was leaving behind me as I said good-bye to old friends and hello to the new life I had prayed for.

Reflections from a Quilter

Gerda Lycklama

We do our good work for others, but we get the blessing from it.

In the early 1970s I was standing in a drug store in Chatham, New Jersey, when I read the poem "Footprints" for the first time. My initial thought was that it was a nice poem. The more I stood and read it, the more meaningful it became. I bought it, brought it home, and put it in my kitchen window, where I could read it daily. We had five small children at the time, and many days I would say, "Lord, carry me. I need to be lifted up."

A year or two later, at a church function, I met a tiny, energetic, red-headed woman named Margaret. We sat next to each other at lunch and, after some small talk, found out that we both came from Ontario, in Canada. She still lived there. In our conversation, I found out that she was the author of "Footprints." Wow!

I was absolutely thrilled to be chatting with her. What a blessing just to ask her questions. Our time was short—other people needed her attention. We did not get to speak to each other again that day, and our lives continued on separately.

Years passed. We moved to California, where we lived for sixteen years. Then, in 1994, we relocated to the northern part of Washington State. My husband and I became involved with our missions committee at a church in Marysville, Washington, and so another door opened up for us. A couple from British Columbia came to one of our mission conferences to present a children's program. They were Paul and Margaret Powers. The names did not register with me, but when we saw each other, we knew we had met before—though where, we couldn't recall.

It took us the entire weekend to figure out that we had met Margaret in New Jersey more than twenty years earlier. We both had moved to the West Coast—the Powers, to British Columbia—and now the Lord was allowing our paths to cross again. This time, we exchanged phone numbers and addresses. I was introduced to Paul, and I knew I had met him somewhere before as well. My husband also knew he had met him. Neither of us could remember where. Paul had written a book, and he gave me a copy to read. Back at home I could hardly wait to dig in and read it. Bingo! All the pieces started to fall into place.

Years before, in the 1960s, when we lived in Ontario, Paul

led a group called Youth for Christ. Before we were married, my husband and I had attended the group on Saturdays—our date night. It was free and, being students, we didn't have much money. We were married in 1964 and later moved to New Jersey.

I phoned Paul and told him the mystery had been solved, and we had a good time reminiscing. Over the past years, I had become a quilter and started a quilting group with a number of women, making quilts for orphans and people in need. Margaret and Paul soon started taking our quilts on their mission trips. We had fun and met in coffee shops, malls, parking lots, and various other spots to deliver the quilts to them—sometimes more than fifty at a time.

Later on, I made a quilt with the "Footprints" poem on it. I just couldn't give it away, so I hung it in our hallway, where I passed it many times a day. Its message still blesses me. I also made a quilt for Margaret, and at one of our later mission conferences gave it to her as a thank-you gift. Tears and hugs followed.

Margaret's poem has meant so much to me and, as my husband and I started our mission trips, I took many copies of the poem with me and shared it with people all over the world. Some copies are in other languages. I explain the meaning of the poem, and I see faces light up when people grasp it.

This poem is powerful. It has brought me great peace, comfort, and joy. Even now that our oldest daughter has been diagnosed with cancer, I say, "Lord, thank You for caring so much. You will carry me and lift me up. You will be there for me, for my daughter, and for our family." We need only to look up and to ask.

Who would have thought so many years ago that, when Margaret wrote this poem at a challenging time in her own life, its meaning would help so many people? I praise and thank the Lord for the gift He gave me in meeting this dear woman. My life has been so much richer because of the "Footprints" poem.

For the Birds

Bill Ross

A chance remark can trigger a memory . . . and warm a heart.

I once read that you get more patient as you age, but that hasn't been the case with me. As I approach my eightieth year, I find I've become stubborn, opinionated and, according to a couple of grandchildren, crotchety.

I've defended my outspokenness with the argument that, after all these many years on God's earth, I've earned the right to speak my mind. I've been widowed twice, retired twice (I have two gold watches for my years in the workforce), and am content living alone in an apartment complex largely populated by my contemporaries.

But I've also noticed that friends aren't phoning as often as they used to, my kids aren't extending invitations other than for oblig-atory holidays, and neighbors smile politely but don't ask me in for a cup of tea. No complaints—I'm perfectly content to put my feet up, watch a baseball game or an old movie, read my newspapers and magazines, and call it a night by 10 p.m.

Mornings, I usually have my coffee and bran cereal, take a walk in the park, and then do a little shopping or visit my friend Max in the hospital. And if people annoy me, I speak my mind. The other day I had to remind two people to pick up after their dogs. And I even walked over to a police car, where two officers were having their coffee and donuts, and told them that it wasn't a smart idea to leave their car idling. They glanced at me with a look of surprise and amusement, but as I continued my walk, cane in hand, I felt I had done my civic duty.

As I said, my grandchildren have noticed this change in my attitude. Years ago, when we were all a good deal younger, I introduced the kids to tennis in the summer and skiing in the winter. I was always a "young" grandpa—they had trouble keeping up with me. The younger of the two, Lindsay, has always loved animals—and I introduced her to pony rides and the magical world of butterflies. We had special days when she and Grandpa would walk to the park and feed the ducks and the birds. I proudly watched as she matured from an excited little girl on a pony into a serious horsewoman. Jason, my grandson, was always an athletic kid. He played to win—and the shelves in his room were cluttered with trophies. But I took pride in the games he lost, too, because that's when he showed his good sportsmanship and his classy side. For a few summers we took driving trips to watch

Major League Baseball games. Somewhere in my cluttered apartment, I have black-and-white photos of the two of us at Boston's Fenway Park and Chicago's Wrigley Field. I should look for them.

Lindsay is now twenty and in college, and Jason, twenty-three, is working as a chef. Their parents have divorced, and I miss the holidays we used to share. I ask the grandkids to come over for lunch, but they're always "too busy." And when they do visit, it's often strained. I lose my patience with their endless texting to friends while I'm trying to have a conversation. I know my current life isn't so interesting to them, and my political opinions don't impress them. Nor did it help when I found myself lecturing to them on the way I was raised versus how easy they have it now. No doubt, I pontificated on the subject more than once. I wasn't amused when I overheard Lindsay telling her mom—my former daughter-in-law—that she had spent a difficult hour with "Raised." Things got progressively worse as I continued to correct Lindsay on everything from her attitude to her grammar.

Now I can't remember how long it's been since I've seen the grandkids. Although the days often drag, the months fly and I lose track of time. Occasionally Jason calls me and we chat for a minute and a half, usually about how our favorite baseball or hockey teams are doing. Lindsay? We've distanced ourselves. I think she inherited my stubborn streak and, after our last painful visit, neither one of us has picked up the phone.

This morning I had my usual breakfast and went for my usual

walk. Then I returned home, had a bowl of soup, and dozed off in front of the TV for half an hour or so. I've always felt routines are important, and today was a shopping day. So I headed to the local market and picked up some bananas, a couple of potatoes, and a piece of fish. Feeling a little hungry, I stopped at the nearby café for a cup of tea and a bran muffin. The place was noisy. Students from the nearby high school and college were lining up for their fancy coffee concoctions—lattes, or whatever they're called. How could they afford them? In my day, we'd be out playing some sport or working at an after-school job. Well, that's the way I was raised.

I sat down with my muffin and tea and watched as the kids tinkered with their cell phones. They all had these devices—reading messages, sending messages. In my day, when we were with friends, we'd talk to each other, for goodness' sake. I shook my head disapprovingly, and I could see several of the students snicker in my direction.

My muffin finished, I stood up and headed for the door. A young man—perhaps my grandson's age—was a few paces ahead of me. I followed him out onto the street and saw him toss some litter onto the pavement. It didn't take me long to catch up to him, and I didn't hesitate to say what was bothering me.

"Excuse me," I said, and he turned in my direction. "Why couldn't you have tossed your garbage into the trash can instead of throwing it on the street?"

I expected some smart or rude reply, yet his smile and polite demeanor took me by surprise.

"Oh, sir," he said politely. "I couldn't agree with you more. It bothers me too to see people litter the streets. But if you look closely," he continued, pointing toward the ground, "you'll see that I tossed some muffin crumbs for the birds. I always try to do that."

For once in my life, I was nearly speechless. "Oh," I mumbled. "You like to feed the birds. Good for you."

I continued on my way home. I realized I wasn't dragging my feet—there was even a bounce to my step. And I found myself smiling as I decided what I'd do as soon as I entered my apartment.

After putting the groceries down, I picked up the phone and dialed. I was happy to hear someone at the other end pick up the receiver—I didn't want to leave a message.

"Hello," said a familiar voice.

"Lindsay?" I replied. "It's Grandpa."

I could tell she wasn't expecting my call, and I continued. "Sweetheart, I'm so sorry I haven't spoken to you for a long while. But honey, you know I love you. And today—today I was thinking about how, when you were a little girl, we'd go to the lake and feed the birds. So—maybe if you have time this weekend, we could have lunch at the park, like in the old days."

I figured she wasn't yet ready for a truce, and I didn't expect much of an answer. She probably had plans to see her friends—

and she wasn't likely to indulge her crotchety grandfather. But after a few moments—probably once the shock wore off—she spoke up, and answered with the little-girl laugh I remembered.

"Oh, Grandpa," she said. "That would be nice. Except—"

"What, Lindsay?" I interrupted.

"Except, Grandpa, I have to ask you something."

"Yes?" I answered. "What do you want to know?"

"Will I bring the breadcrumbs, or will you?"

PART EIGHT
Old Favorites

WE ARE PLEASED to include favorite stories from earlier books as a bonus section. They all reflect the theme of the *Treasury*. At the beginning of each one, I explain what the story means to me and why I chose to include it.

Footprints of Faith

Margaret Fishback Powers

This tribute to my mother was written in 1998 and presented as the Mother's Day Conference Message at the JOY (Just Older Youth) Club, Blue Mountain Baptist Church, in Coquitlam, British Columbia. It appeared in *Footprints for Mothers and Daughters* (2011). I hope you like its message, which continues to remind me of the daily need for compassion toward others.

Several weeks ago, I picked up cards at a Hallmark store. I was under stress. I had made my own cards until the day I married, and continued doing so throughout the years as wife and mother. I felt that I was the only one who could put together just the right words for my loved ones. Now, I had suddenly turned to store-bought cards. My tear-filled eyes scanned Get Well, Birthday, Miss You, Baby Shower, Congratulations, and Sympathy shelves. Then I spotted a Mother's Day card that was beautiful and seemed to say all the right words I wanted to say to my mother. It was too late. I showed it to my husband, and he gently reminded me that my dear Mum didn't need to read how we felt about her. She had just passed on to Glory, only a few months previously. He told me that my handmade cards had probably meant more to her than all these lovely store items.

As we reread the card, I wondered if I had shared all these glowing tributes to her, face to face. Had I told her how much I appreciated the hours she spent cooking and trying to teach me to cook? How much it meant to learn the importance of making a sudden surprise overnight guest feel comfortable and welcome in our home? She would always say, "Anyone can have a house, but it takes extra love and care to make it a home."

How I had missed her encouragement and smiling face when I left for teachers' college and university. Then, when I left for northern Quebec, I really missed her. But she never failed to write, and I still have a beautiful box of her letters, with ribbons and bows to tie it up; her handwritten words give me comfort. I treasure the times spent with her—in the fields, hoeing; in the garden, weeding and chatting; or out in the barn, looking at new-born animals or gathering eggs. She would relate stories of her family history, of her parents, grandparents, and great-grandparents, and tell of those special talents they had been given, and their walk of faith. Mum passed on "tales of a path well worn."

She often said, "Just like women of the Old and New Testament, we too must walk by faith that new path ahead, and mark it well for those who follow by faith in our footprints."

It was not easy to follow in Mum's footprints of faith—footprints that she walked daily in the sight of the Lord. She was so consistent, so unconditionally loving to her family and friends, and faithful to her last day on earth. Her trust was like a new piece of ground to be cleared, tilled, prepared, and seeded. She wanted a good harvest, and I believe her daughters have called her blessed, as we read in Proverbs 32:28.

I talked to my mum by telephone long-distance a few hours before her going home, and if I had known that it was to be our last conversation, I would have kept her talking all night. I can't talk to her now, but I must try to transfer her recipe for a walk of faith to my daughters and granddaughters and let them know that Mum left deep footprints for us to follow.

Their Faith Strengthened

Agnes Manthorpe

This story is from *Footprints for Mothers and Daughters* (2011), which celebrates the special bond between two generations. My friend Agnes reminds us that there are times when we must hold back on a plan to be with a loved one—in this case, to strengthen the bond in a personal relationship. As a result of our constraint, we may be doubly blessed later on.

When our daughter, Marthe, gave birth, my husband, Ross, and I were naturally excited to welcome our first grandchild. We planned to fly to England to welcome him into the family. Then we received the news that the baby had contracted meningitis and was in intensive care.

My friend Sally gave me some wise advice: she suggested that we *not* go, allowing my daughter time to be with her husband. We agreed, and felt that our decision would give the parents an opportunity for their faith to be strengthened while we all hoped for a miracle. We would let Marthe and Ray face this extremely serious situation alone with God.

Two days later, Marthe called with extraordinary news. "Mother," she said, her voice soaring with happiness, "you won't believe it!" The doctor who was looking after Andrew had been involved in the original research—carried out in Toronto—for the medication used to treat meningitis. "Andrew is going to be all right."

Every day, for forty-two days after the discovery of the illness, that doctor checked on our little grandson. Today, Andrew is a healthy six-foot-one young man who serves the Lord.

Family

Joni Eareckson Tada

Joni Eareckson Tada is an evangelical Christian author, host, and founder of Joni and Friends, an organization "accelerating Christian ministry in the disability community." She is the author of more than thirty-five books on the subjects of disability and Christianity.

A diving accident in 1967 left Joni hospitalized and paralyzed. After two years of rehabilitation and in a wheelchair, she began working to help others in similar situations. She wrote of her experiences in her internationally bestselling autobiography, *Joni*, which has been distributed in many languages and was made into a feature film of the same name.

From *Footprints for Mothers and Daughters* (2011), Joni's story reminds us that sometimes God has a different plan in mind for His children, although it is often hard to understand at the time. In this case, God wanted Joni and Ken to be parents to many needy and broken children.

For years, Ken and I tried to conceive a child. I knew of other spinal-cord-injured women who had given birth to children, and I was convinced I could do the same. I planned to turn my art studio into a nursery and my wheelchair into a "stroller." I could even envision holding my baby girl in a kangaroo carrier on my wheelchair. But it wasn't to be. After many tests at an infertility clinic, Ken and I realized we would not be able to have a child.

At first, I was devastated. But then we realized that we already had a family—a worldwide family. We began to rejoice anew over the thousands of spiritual children, especially little girls with disabilities, who had been touched by my story over the years. Ken and I began to pray in a deeper, more specific way for these young people. Almost overnight God took away my pain and the emptiness of my barren womb.

Guideposts

Margaret Fishback Powers

This essay appeared in *Footprints: Scripture with Reflections Inspired by the Best-Loved Poem* (1998) one of my series of "little books." As I reread it, I am reminded that God is ever present for every age, to lighten our burden and give joy to the heart. At times, it seems that "Footprints" never grows old and thus appears timeless, and new, to a first-time reader. No matter the week, month, or year, burdens continue to fall on all of us at various times of our lives. I feel that we can confidently approach the Good Shepherd and ask to leave that burden, great or small, on Him.

Every now and then during our devotional time, my husband, Paul, and I reread the poem I wrote for him back in 1964. During these times of renewal and prayer, we talk over the events of our lives and share burdens we have for ourselves and others.

Very often, we realize that the Great Shepherd has once again reached out and carried us through the day as we spend these introspective moments together.

If the pleasure of sharing these thoughts has taught us anything, it is this: that God's Word is true. Our Heavenly Father is faithful and will never leave us or forsake us. As we come to Him daily, willing to be shaped and directed, His Word gives guideposts of clear direction. Almost everything we read, see, and experience shows us in some way that, although we do not visibly see God, He is with us. Over centuries of time, others have looked back to understand that God's Spirit and presence were there, even when they felt alone.

In our quiet moments of reflection, in the fellowship of others, and even in dreams, God opens the doors to our hearts. This is what happened when I originally wrote the poem "Footprints." After hours of wrestling with the darkness of doubt and despair, I finally surrendered to Him and, in the early morning light of peace, wrote the poem as a result of that spiritual experience.

Listen for the gentle stirring of God's grace in your own mind . . . Each of us is different in our spiritual need, just as each of our days is different. God wants to place His signature on your life in a unique way. As you spend time, even just a few moments each day, reflecting on *His Word*, it will help you to know Him better.

Spiritual growth is not so much what we have done, but the

feeling of love for Him we put into everything we do. It is not so much in knowing about God that we grow, but in getting to know Him in a personal way. It is in becoming "a friend of God" as Abraham did that we grow in His grace, talking with Him as our companion along the way.

Words of Encouragement

Margaret Fishback Powers

These reflections appeared in *Footprints: Scripture with Reflections Inspired by the Best-Loved Poem* (1998). I hope that some of the thoughts that I wrote down so many years ago will provide comfort today.

We all go through times when life seems to overwhelm us. The Bible reassures us that God's presence is with us to help us, even when we don't realize it. Moments of darkness in our lives may be caused by the death of a loved one, the loss of a job or home, or another great tragedy of life. Yet there is a greater darkness than these tragedies: the darkness in the eyes of one who has not felt God's love and grace, and the assurance of His hope. There is hope for all of us. There is light.

⚘

I HAVE A FRIEND who loves to take long walks with me. We talk and laugh and enjoy each other's company as we stroll along. The exercise is beneficial, and so is the conversation. The Lord is a lot like my friend. He enjoys walking with us as our companion on life's pathway. And He brings blessings into our lives when we walk closely with Him. The awareness of God's presence with us is encouraging and heartwarming. It is as if we were two friends seated beside a rippling brook, enjoying a gentle breeze on a warm spring afternoon.

⚘

EVEN WHEN WE ARE surrounded by family and friends, some problems seem to double in size of their own accord. If we toss and turn in the early morning hours thinking about them, they become ten times as large. Yet though it seems the whole world has gone wrong around us, we are not alone—God is with us.

⚘

WHEN WE LIVE WITH an attitude that looks back over our lives with regret and "if only," we rob ourselves of hope. We rob ourselves of the joy of God's grace. God never changes. He is the

God of grace. He is the God of hope. He is the God of love who offers us a life free of regrets. When we have experienced God's forgiveness, we are new creatures. We do not need to live a life of regrets.

TODDLERS OFTEN FACE SEPARATION ANXIETY—a feeling of abandonment whenever their parents leave the room. Though we may be much older and wiser than little children, we still feel the pain of loneliness and isolation. Both Jesus and the psalmist also knew what it was to feel alone, abandoned, forgotten . . . When loneliness overtakes us, we need to remember that we are *not alone*. God has promised to be with us.

WE MUST REMEMBER to listen closely to God's voice when trouble rages around us. When the agonies of life begin to crush us, God has not moved away from us. Often we have moved away from Him. We need to return to Him in faith and call on Him for His strength. Whether we face death, discouragement, loss, or pain, we can take great comfort in knowing that no sorrow is too deep that God cannot feel it with us. And God wants to help deliver us from it. He wants to bring us to His divine comfort.

WHEN WE NEED DIRECTION, we must trust that the Lord will take our faith, limited as it is, and make something of lasting value out of it. God has a plan for us. He cares about our dilemmas, hears our heartfelt cries, and will answer us in ways that will astonish us and fill our hearts with songs of joy.

RUTS AND POTHOLES; shadows and deep darkness: the journey of life can sometimes be very troubling. We stumble and have difficulty following in God's footsteps. We are fearful of the unknown. But God's Word reminds us to trust, to believe, to hope. We all go through troubling times, but we must never doubt God's presence with us. Those things we consider difficulties are often God's opportunities for our greater blessing. We must trust, believe, hope, and continue to walk the path he has laid before us.

THE CREATOR OF THE UNIVERSE calls me his child—what a blessing! What a privilege! What a responsibility!

Hand in Hand

Margaret Fishback Powers

This commentary appeared in *Life's Little Inspiration Book* (1994). I still carry a copy of that book in my briefcase as a companion to my Bible when traveling. It perks me up when I feel down, and it doesn't take a lot of room in the outside pocket. It continues to hold a special place in my heart because it reminds me of home, my mum, and the different places and people involved when I wrote particular passages. Incidents that inspire me involve comfort, companionship, and compassion—for and from others—to give me courage to carry on. I appreciate the kindness and thoughtfulness of others, and I hope that I am never too busy or distracted to acknowledge people. One person I am often reminded of is my friend Jody Bergsma. You'll find a new story by Jody on page 62.

A friend of ours, Jody Bergsma, is an artist. She did the artwork for a small card we carry in our Bibles. It shows a mother and child walking along hand in hand. The caption reads, "Parents hold their children's hand for a while . . . their hearts forever." This is the way it is with our relationship with the Lord. We may let go, but He keeps us in His heart forever. And if, as we walk through life, we feel that God is not there, who has moved? Not God. He has promised, "I will never leave you." To follow in the Lord's footsteps, we need help, humor, and humility. Who would argue that this world needs plenty of comfort and cheer?

God's Unknown Ways

Margaret Fishback Powers

These words appeared in *The Footprints Book of Prayers* (1996), a book used by me and others over the years. As I travel, during breaks in meet-and-greet book-signing tours, I've been surprised to meet a number of people who had copies on hand or knew of my books. Some had even heard me in a radio interview or seen me on television. They would often mention that "Footprints" was in their prayer book, or was available at the local Christian bookstore, and some would ask me to sign their personal copy. I believe that prayer helps us see some of the many unexpected ways in which God works behind the scenes of our daily lives. It is like a fine, invisible thread that silently weaves its way in and through our lives to blend into a tapestry of joy, where people can see His beauty.

The importance of giving away bookmarks or one of my books to comfort or encourage someone cannot be overstated. I hope they will provide comfort, or encourage people to perhaps contact me or a pastor, to share a personal experience in prayer, and to find the peace that they long for.

"In all your ways acknowledge Him, and He shall direct your paths" (Proverbs 3:6). I memorized this Bible verse many years ago, but I never really knew its meaning until one day in 1980.

We decided to move the family from Ontario to British Columbia, a great distance, as we felt there would be more opportunities for our work with children. We were not even halfway there when we discovered that we had miscalculated our funds. Now, I will admit that we had stayed an extra night in the Banff Springs Hotel, mainly because a very special friend was working there, but, among other things, we were using far more fuel than we expected to need.

By the time we crossed the border into British Columbia and arrived at Rogers Pass, there was some doubt in our minds about whether this move was really God's direction at all. Funds were at an all-time low and, with four people sleeping and traveling in the van, things got a bit testy. In the morning, we stopped for breakfast at a café and decided to order two breakfasts to share among the four of us.

As we held hands to pray, Paul explained to the children that we would have to cut back from then on, since we had to put so much more money into gas than we had anticipated. Our eldest daughter replied, "Dad, if God is really leading us, He will provide for us." We gave thanks and started to eat. What we didn't know was that the family sitting opposite us was watching us. There had evidently been harsh and loud angry words on their holiday, and the father was threatening to turn their motor home around and go back home. They watched us for a while, and, although we kept our conversations very quiet, they must have overheard us discuss our finances and our expressions of faith in God. Eventually they got up and left the restaurant.

As we prepared to leave, the waitress at the desk told us our bill had been paid by the family who had sat near us. When we came out to the gas station, the attendant invited us to come and fill the van with gas and a liter of oil. It had been paid for in advance!

Never Will I Leave You

Margaret Fishback Powers

The very personal events told here continue to resonate throughout the world as people share with others through books, eBooks, letters, and emails. I chose to open *Footprints: The True Story Behind the Poem That Inspired Millions* (2012, updated edition) with the waterfall event, since it has made a great impact on my life and reminds us of the urgency to share hope and freedom from fear. You'll see that the closing words of the story are from Hebrews 13:5, "Never will I leave you; never will I forsake you." They are just as important to me now as they were all those years ago.

"Oh, it's always so good to be home." I sighed as I said this, looking at Paul, my husband, who was stretched out, relaxing. We'd been woken up early by the birds outside our window.

"Make the most of it, Margie," he responded, "we'll be off again tomorrow."

"Where to, this time?" I asked, weariness sounding in my voice.

"Vancouver."

We'd just returned from a two-month series of church camps in Washington State. Summer was always our busiest season. Our Little People's Ministry, which was dedicated to evangelism—to equipping and encouraging children to learn and grow spiritually—found us hopping from one camp, church, and crusade to another. Not that it wasn't challenging and fulfilling; of course it was; in fact, it was one of the dreams of our lives come true—but toward the middle of the summer, we were more than ready to kick back and relax at our home in Coquitlam, British Columbia.

Now it was August. As I looked at our travel itinerary, observing the date—Monday, August 7, 1989, a Canadian holiday—I thought we would at least sleep in. I didn't know it at the time, but the date was to be forever imprinted in our memories—an unforgettable day with triple events that will be seared in our minds for life.

It was still very early that Monday morning when the phone rang. "I'll get it; stay put," I said to my husband.

"Hi, Mom, how's everything?"

"It's Paula." I mouthed the words to Paul. "Everything's fine,"

I assured our daughter, "but we were just saying how good it felt to be home."

"Well, in that case, maybe I shouldn't ask you this," she said, then hesitated. It was only a momentary pause. "How would you like to drive a carload of kids up to Golden Ears and picnic at the Lower Falls?" Paula knew what pushovers we were for kids. Golden Ears was a vast provincial park about ten miles away. "I need an extra vehicle—someone dropped out." She paused briefly again. "If you'll do it, the sooner you can come and meet us at the church, the better. Everyone's waiting. They're anxious to get this show on the road."

I glanced at Paul. "Okay, we'll come," I promised. I already knew what Paul's reaction would be. There just wasn't anything he wouldn't do for kids; his own childhood had been so traumatic.

"Thanks, Mom, I knew I could count on you and Dad. Bring your swimsuit and wear your shorts."

I quickly pulled on my swimsuit, slipped a pair of shorts over it, and reached for the top and shirt jacket I'd worn the day before. "I'll leave all this stuff where it is," I said, remembering everything in the pockets.

"Yes, don't take time to clean out your pockets," Paul said. A few minutes later we were on our way out the door. As we drove the short distance to the church where Paula and the kids were waiting, I checked inside the pockets of the shirt jacket, fingering the bottle of Paul's heart pills and another bottle of extra-strength Tylenol.

Why do I always load myself down with this stuff? I asked myself.

We did a quick drive-through at McDonald's on our way out of town, the back of the van filled with kids. "Golden Ears Park, here we come!" one of the kids shouted, and we all laughed. It was going to be a fun day. We enjoyed being with Paula and her young charges. We often jokingly said to each other and our friends that our daughters, Tina and Paula, and their young friends kept us on our toes. There's no time to think about advancing years when you're around young people.

"What a gorgeous day," I said. Everyone agreed that they'd picked the right day. Twice before, the outing had been canceled because of inclement weather—British Columbia's liquid sunshine.

Upon arrival at the park, we joined the others clambering out of cars. A few instructions to the group from Paula about the need to be careful—the rocks would be slippery, and we'd be crossing the top of Lower Falls on a rock ledge—and we all took off. Just before leaving, Paula explained, "Now listen, you guys, there's a forty-foot-deep glacier pool off one side. No funny stuff, okay?"

We were proud of our beautiful daughter. She had such a love for young people, and she and her sister had always been a part of our work with youth. They were extremely gifted ventriloquists, and it was a delight to be around them. Now, I watched Paula lead the kids, her long strawberry-blonde hair swinging free as we approached the rock ledge walkway.

We all made our way cautiously across the slippery rocks and then found perches for ourselves as we paused to rest and enjoy the breathtakingly beautiful scenery. We watched rather anxiously as some older fellows (not part of our group) dove into the glacier pool from high atop a rock perch. "That water is ice-cold," I called to Paula. "How can they stand it?"

"I don't know," she called back, shaking her head. "I'm glad it's not me."

Paul elected to stay on the other side of the glacier pool, where there was another, smaller pocket of water that looked inviting. He had said to me, "This is where I'm going to read." I knew he wanted to prepare for the Vancouver meetings. He carefully made his way around to where he could enjoy the beauty and have some seclusion.

We saw lots of swimmers and sunbathers enjoying themselves on the rocks and in the water. Looking down from the ledge so high up, we could see others amusing themselves at the base of the falls and in the river. I couldn't help thinking that there should be barricades or fences, and signs warning people that it was dangerous and slippery in places.

"It's so beautiful up here," one of the girls remarked.

"Absolutely heavenly," I replied, thinking to myself that it felt as if we were so close to heaven that we could almost reach up and touch God. Spruce and pine trees towered above us, the sun filtering through. The glacier water was emerald-green.

After sunning a while, I looked at my watch and called across to my husband, "Paul, it's a quarter past two." Paul glanced up from his reading and acknowledged that he'd heard me.

Just then, Paula said, "I'm going back across to where Dad is. She started out over the rock ledge. At the same time somewhere nearby, a dog barked, startling me.

As a mother, I thought about the sixty-eight-foot falls on the one side and the forty-foot-deep glacier pool on the other, and called out, cautioning Paula, "Oh, be careful." I watched as she inched her way along. Paul was also watching as she made her way. He stood up and held out his hand to reach for her when she got closer. At that moment she missed her footing and fell into a whirlpool of water. It sucked her into its vortex, spinning her around three times, and before any of us knew what was happening, she was spun out and over the falls.

Everyone was screaming. I jumped to my feet, screaming, too. I couldn't help Paula. What should I do? I glanced across at my husband and saw him clutch his chest and fall. At that moment, I knew he was having a heart attack—I could actually see his color change. It was all happening as if in slow motion, but the confusion was terrible, and I feared for the lives of the other young people if they should panic. I turned my back momentarily to face the kids, who were hysterical. "We must pray," I shouted, crying out, "O God, help us!"

I reached around my neck for a necklace that Paul had given me on our twenty-third wedding anniversary just the year before. I glanced down at the eagle mounted on black onyx and sent a telegram-prayer heavenward. "Lord, if You are going to take Paula, take her without too much pain, and O God, spare my husband."

I thought my daughter must surely be dead. How could anyone survive a sixty-eight-foot fall into glacier-cold water? I knew I had to get to my husband, but I instinctively also knew I couldn't trust my shaky legs to the slippery rock ledge. Just as I was about to enter the water to swim across, a man called to me from where my husband was. "I'm going to throw this rope across the pool. My son is alongside you; he'll grab it. Hang on to the rope as you swim across."

What I didn't know was that the man's wife was a nurse who was at that very moment administering aid to Paul. Earlier that day, as they left home, the man had grabbed the rope that they used to tether their dog, and his son had said to him, "What are you doing with that rope?" "I don't know," he'd replied as he stuck it in his pocket. Now I was holding on to the rope with one hand as I swam with the other. The water was icy cold, but I was oblivious to the temperature as I made my way across.

Down below, some boys on the rocks at the base of the falls saw a body floating by and, thinking it was a corpse, pulled it ashore. A woman sunning on the rocks observed all this, rushed over, and immediately began resuscitation. I found out later that this woman was a nurse trained specifically in drowning accidents.

I struggled onto the rocks, anxious to reach my husband's side, the man who had been holding the rope helping me. But somehow, in my desperate and frantic attempt, I slipped several times on the slimy rocks and broke my right arm. It hung limp at my side, and as soon as I was out of the water, I was aware of excruciating pain. Then I saw a woman bending over Paul. The man told me, "She's a nurse, trained in cardiac arrest."

"Thank God," I murmured, my whole body shaking uncontrollably. Suddenly I remembered Paul's heart medicine and told the nurse that in my left pocket was a bottle of Nitrol. Someone noticed me trembling and thoughtfully threw a large towel around me.

At one point, the nurse turned and calmly said, "They tell me that it's your daughter who went over the falls. My sister-in-law is down below; she's a nurse trained in water rescue."

I fell back on the rocks, overcome with emotions, grateful to think that perhaps Paula had been rescued. I was just about to pass out when I heard the nurse add, "Oh, it's too bad we don't have some pain medicine." I tried reaching into my right pocket but could only motion.

"She's a walking pharmacy," the woman said as she found my bottle of extra-strength Tylenol.

The presence of both these nurses was amazing, but they explained that they were on strike at the provincial hospitals, which was why they were at the park on an outing. One of the swimmers we'd seen diving was also a long-distance runner. He immediately took off, running to reach the nearest phone and call in ambulances for help. Somehow the kids all carefully made their way back to the cars, waiting and praying while anxiously wondering what was to be the outcome of all this.

A search-and-rescue team arrived first and was already starting to carry us out when the ambulances came. Stretchers were then brought in. Four hours after the accidents, we were in the emergency room at Maple Ridge General Hospital. At three in the morning I learned that X-rays revealed that Paula had a broken neck, her arm had been pulled out of its socket, and she had a perforated kidney and liver. She was a gravely injured young woman, but she was alive.

Nearby, in the intensive-care ward, my husband lay hooked to heart monitors and intravenous tubes. A few hours later a nurse came and asked him, "Mr. Powers, would you like me to pray for you, your daughter, and your wife?" He nodded yes, and so she prayed.

When she finished praying, she said, "I think it would help you if I read a little piece I have here in my pocket," and she pulled out a card. Holding my husband's hand, she quietly read:

One night I dreamed a dream.
I was walking along the beach with my Lord.
Across the dark sky flashed scenes from my life.
For each scene, I noticed two sets

of footprints in the sand,
one belonging to me
and one to my Lord.

When the last scene of my life shot before me
I looked back at the footprints in the sand.
There was only one set of footprints.
I realized that this was at the lowest
and saddest times of my life.
This always bothered me
and I questioned the Lord
about my dilemma.

"Lord, You told me when I decided to follow You,
You would walk and talk with me all the way.
But I'm aware that during the most troublesome
times of my life there is only one set of footprints.
I just don't understand why, when I needed You most,
You leave me."

He whispered, "My precious child,
I love you and will never leave you,
never, ever, during your trials and testings.
When you saw only one set of footprints,
it was then that I carried you."

When the nurse finished reading, she looked at my husband and said, "I don't know the author; it's anonymous."

Paul lifted his hand very weakly and said, "I do. I know the author." The nurse thought he wasn't fully conscious because of the medication he'd been given, but Paul said, "I know the author very well . . . she's my wife."

WITH MY HUSBAND and daughter in hospital beds, both in intensive care, and with my arm in a cast, the landscape of our lives seemed overshadowed by a dark sky. Yet Paul and Paula were alive, miraculously so, and I knew from past experience that during this troublesome time we would be carried. God had carried us before; He would carry us now.

TODAY, PAULA, our youngest daughter, is thriving. As we have reflected on this major event in our lives, we realized that God was speaking to us again and reminding us that He would never leave us or forsake us. He is there all the time while we are going through the difficulties, and He will help us carry on. Many times over the years of ministry, that single event has come back to our minds to encourage us. The message that appears in various books throughout the Scripture is wonderfully expressed in Hebrews 13:5, "Never will I leave you; never will I forsake you."

It is just as important to me today.

A Beautiful Song

Tony Campolo

This story appeared in *Footprints: Scripture with Reflections for Teens* (2004). Over the years I've been delighted to hear about the impact the reflections in that book have had on young people.

A friend of mine, the chaplain of a college, was brokenhearted when he found out that one of his brightest students, a Christian, had been hit by a bus and killed. One upset student asked my friend, "Why did Jesus kill Cliff?" My friend answered, "You're an intelligent person. You ought to be able to tell the difference between Jesus and a bus!"

While God doesn't make bad things happen, the Bible promises us that in the midst of bad things, God works to bring good out of it all (see Romans 8:28). I remember a guy who had his own TV show. And one of the other guys on the show, José Melos, was a fantastic piano player. Sometimes the show host would walk over to the piano and slap his hands down on a bunch of keys. They made an awful sound, of course. Then he would say, "OK, José, let's see what you can make out of that mess!"

José would then put his fingers on the exact keys the show host had "played" and build those sounds into a magnificent melody. Incredibly, the clashing sounds became a beautiful song.

God can do that with the messes in our lives. God is able to take our tragedies, and the mistakes we make, and turn them into something beautiful.

Growing Up

Molly Detweiler

This is another story from *Footprints: Scripture with Reflections for Teens* (2004). We're reminded that no matter our age, we will always be God's children.

When I was a little girl, I used to pray about everything. If I was climbing up a tree and suddenly realized I couldn't get down, I would ask God to help me. If my stomach hurt, I would ask God to heal it. If my cat was lost, I would ask God to find her. And sometimes, I just sat on my swing in the backyard and sang God a song to tell Him I loved Him.

Then, I grew up. I still prayed, but mostly just for the "big" things—a relative who had cancer or a missionary who was being persecuted. Somewhere between the ages of ten and twenty, I decided that I could handle the "little things" on my own and that God knew I loved him—I didn't need to sit in the backyard and sing anymore.

Recently, though, I've begun to realize that growing up doesn't mean that you stop "bothering" God with little prayers or that you praise Him only at church on Sunday. Does a good dad want his child to stop coming to him for advice and love once the child grows up? No!

God never stops wanting to hear from us about every aspect of our lives, and I imagine He is sad when we lose that "childlike faith" we once had and start carrying all our troubles on our own.

So, while we must all grow up, we never have to stop being God's child. I think I'll go into the backyard and sing Him a song . . . just to say thanks.

The Minefield

Margaret Fishback Powers

Over many years, we have received news about or spoken personally to military personnel whose lives were dramatically affected by a "Footprints" situation. Once, in Yuma, Arizona, after the book table had closed for the night, a soldier about to leave for front-line duty was desperate to purchase two books, one autographed for her mom and one for her. She needed these books urgently—she had a feeling that she would not return. Before coming home, we saw on television that she had in fact made the ultimate sacrifice.

Once in a while, an event is reported on TV or in the newspaper that refers to "Footprints" in an eye-catching way. Following the 1990–91 Persian Gulf crisis, Paul and I were on a meet-and-greet book-signing tour to the Maritime provinces (and also celebrating our twenty-fifth wedding anniversary). Our daughter Paula, in her early years of recovery, was with us.

She felt she was walking lightly, step by step each day, over her personal minefield and wondering when she would explode with pain and shock, or if she'd make it through.

One day, I picked up the morning newspaper from Bangor, Maine, and the following story melted my heart. It appeared in *Footprints: Scripture with Reflections for Men* (2004).

A young, self-effacing marine from Tennessee who had risked his life in an Iraqi minefield. He miraculously survived. The next morning, the tankers and their crew studied the terrain, and found seven mines and some tripwires alongside his footprints. They told him he was either the stupidest or the luckiest marine alive.

Lance-Corporal Mark Schrader told his buddies, and later the media, "I didn't see any tripwires!" Afterward, squad members talked about the incident and someone mentioned the poem "Footprints." "It was obviously not my footprints that went through that minefield," the young hero maintains. "It was God. He carried me."

That story alone has made it all worthwhile . . .

What God has done for me, what He did for the young marine, God will do for anyone who asks Him to walk with them through life.

"I am the Lord, the God of all mankind. Is anything too hard for me?" (Jeremiah 32:27).

The Physics Class

Showey Yazdanian

Stepping back in the footprints of time, I have reflected on stories that have moved me to tears, have humbled me to see the love and devotion of a parent, or have caused me to burst out with laughter. This is one of those very "charming and chuckling" stories that tickled my ribcage and reminded me of the difficult recovery time for our daughter Paula, when I anxiously wondered how I could help her. I was so desperate at one point that I joined her university-level poetry class for one semester, only to find that the professor did not get past the discussion of vowels and the myriad daily sounds in our world—which somehow led to the development of poetry. As a result, I quietly dropped out of the course the moment our daughter was able to drive her car again. This story appeared in *Footprints for Mothers and Daughters* (2011).

Night school. The drone of a lecture in the darkness; students a little surly, a little soiled with the day's dust and sweat; teachers a little gray, a little grim as they too hurriedly gulped at tuna sandwiches and warmed-over pasta at break time. There was little pleasure in it for any of us, but that was night school. We all needed something. The teachers needed a little extra money; I needed one last high school credit to graduate on schedule.

It was Dad who usually picked us up from night school. Outside, it was dark and cold, and we would huddle in the narrow corridor and watch like owls for the yellow headlights of the old '86 station wagon. "There it is! The car! The car!" we would yell, and madly clamber into it. Free for another week.

At home there was a warm kitchen, a hot dinner, and a bone-crushing hug from the cuddliest, most devoted mother in the world. There was dinner until homework and homework until bedtime, and that was life twice a week until the night that Mr. Heald, our night school teacher, made an announcement. "Guys," he said. "I know that this could be hard on some of you, but I think it's fair to tell you that we might have to cancel physics this year."

My heart sank. I absolutely couldn't lose this credit.

"But why?" asked my sister.

"I'm sorry, guys," said Mr. Heald mildly when he saw ten faces fall. "The powers that be don't like the low enrolment in this course." Then he turned around and delivered a lecture on momentum. Physics was tough, and Mr. Heald didn't help. He was a nice man with a head of snowy white waves, but his voice was the dull, neutral buzz of a fluorescent light bulb. By break time that night, two people were serenely asleep.

We were morose that night. "What's wrong, darlings? said Mum. We told her.

"But you were on schedule to graduate this year," said Dad, frowning.

"I know that," I said bleakly.

"They'll cancel the class just like that?" asked Dad.

"How should I know?" I returned, a little grouchy. It had been a long night.

"Well," said Mum, with her habitual good cheer. "Perhaps things will improve next week."

I recalled Mr. Heald's soporific classroom and shook my head. "I doubt it."

And they didn't. The following week, enrolment in Mr. Heald's night physics class had dropped to six. Six! We sat in the class-room like a handful of peanuts in an enormous nutshell and listened glumly to another lecture about momentum. "This is it, guys," said Mr. Heald at break time. "Seven is the absolute bare-bones minimum. If we don't get at least one more person by next week, class is permanently dismissed. I'm really sorry."

We were crestfallen. It seems funny, now that I am so irreversibly ensconced in adulthood, but we were as sober as midnight when we broke the news to our parents.

"Don't worry, sausage-mausage," said Mum kindly, with her usual impeccable enunciation. "It's not the end of the world."

"Nothing ever works out," I said. The grievances of a teenager are absolute. "Now I'll never graduate on time. No one will ever sign up for physics, especially not night physics and especially not with Healdy teaching it."

"Healdy?" queried Mum.

"Mr. Heald," I moaned. "The boring physics teacher."

"Right," said Mum thoughtfully. "Mr. Heald."

Next week, when Dad herded us into the car for night school, there was an unexpected passenger in the station wagon.

"Mum, what are you doing here?" I asked. "You never drive to night school with us."

Mum grinned like a green-eyed Cheshire cat. "I've enrolled in night school," she announced.

"What?" my sister and I chorused, in unison.

"Don't worry, petals. Your father called the school's night administration and they'll register me tonight. I'll just have to pop into the office. This should pick up the enrolment a bit, shouldn't it?"

"This is unbelievable!" I exclaimed.

The car scraped into the school parking lot. "Bye, kids," said Dad cheerfully.

"Come along, petals," bustled Mum, gathering up a clipboard and pen. "I don't want to be late for class."

Mr. Heald lingered for a moment over Mum's registration form. "You're not their mother, are you?" he asked her.

"I certainly am, Mr. Heald," beamed Mum in her magnificent accent. "Isn't it lovely—my girls can help me catch up with what I missed. And may I please have last week's homework assignment?"

"Of course," he said, amused but not overly perturbed, and began to lecture about coefficients of friction.

At break time we pestered him for a verdict.

"Sir! Sir! Do we stay or go?"

"Enrolment is up," he said, as inscrutable as ever. "I'll present the case to the administration as attractively as possible."

"Clip a twenty-dollar bill to it, sir!" hooted someone.

"Do your homework," he retorted, and ambled toward the office.

I usually hid in the corridor during break time, assiduously avoiding everybody but my sister, but Mum was unflappable. "Good evening," she enunciated to whomever she met. "I'm Olga. And what's your name?"

Her unaffected charm was irresistible. By the end of break, she was deep in confessional conversation with a young Portuguese boy named Hervoje, who was troubled in love. By the end of class, she was peppering Mr. Heald with questions about gravity.

One week later, Mr. Heald announced, to considerable fanfare, that we would be allowed to finish the semester in peace. Mum joined us two or three more times after that and then quietly dropped the course. She was a diligent and curious student of physics, but the reality of the matter was that she had a full-time job, a husband, and two more children at home. Mr. Heald sincerely encouraged her to stay, but he was a wise old man and I think he knew the truth all along: that Mum's enrolment in high school physics was an act of courage and of some scholarship—but above all, it was an act of love.

Four Generations

Frieda Zink

During our walk of faith, we sometimes walk along paths that seem to run downhill, with bends and twists that confuse us and appear to lead nowhere. Then, suddenly, another path appears that reveals something spectacular. I believe the life story of Frieda is an example of such a path and reveals the incredible miracles God has performed on her journey. At Art and Frieda's sixtieth wedding anniversary celebration, I was reminded that God has nudged them step by step through some very dark periods, then back into the sunlight of joy. One of Frieda's favorite quotes is "you can't have winners without losers." She is funny and talented and elegant, and I have always admired her. Through her Christian code, her impeccable taste, and her positive attitude in spite of physical hardship, Frieda has always been a great example to her family and her friends. This is Frieda's story, from *Footprints for Mothers and Daughters* (2011).

My name is Frieda. I would like to share my story in four distinct parts: grandparents, parents, my childhood and young adulthood, and then marriage and motherhood. I trust you will be encouraged to find hope for the next generation.

Grandparents. My parents came from Ukraine in 1928, during the Depression. My mother's father had a mixed farm and a flour-mill during the Stalin regime. A Ukrainian friend who worked for the government informed my grandfather that the Communists were planning to confiscate his farm. My father had married my mother when she was barely seventeen. She experienced a luxurious honeymoon at her in-laws' farm, where several girls did the housework and cooking, while she did spinning, knitting, and embroidery work. When my grandparents decided to leave their farm and go to Canada, my grandfather insisted that my mother and father go with them.

Parents. My father was a strong man—determined to regain what he had lost in the old country. He knew no English, which made it very difficult for him in his first job of shoveling coal for the railway. But this story is about my mother. She now had to wash his sooty clothes on a washboard, after melting snow to get soft water. Not a pleasant job! For a brief time, until she was expecting her first child, Mother worked at a sewing factory. Then she stayed home. They now had enough food and were safe from Communist rule. They even had Ukrainian neighbors who lived about four miles away. Our house was not warm and was mainly heated by a wood stove. Mother cooked on it, and baked bread in the oven. The stove also had a water tank on the side and a warming oven. My mother was not happy on the farm, since looking after cattle and hogs and doing the grain farming was a lot of work. How does a mother learn to become integrated as a Canadian citizen—learn the English language, learn to make friends?

Childhood and young adulthood. I remember my mother doing wash on the washboard, when I was about four or five years old, and complaining about it to my father, even though he was working with the horses in the field. At one point I felt the lash because I got wet and dirty. However, I do remember my father coming home with a basket of peaches and giving me one. He had been away for a month, working at threshing for a family in Manitoba. I vividly remember my father crying when four cows were killed on a railway track that crossed our farm behind the barn. I saw that my mother faced many challenges and was overwhelmed by them.

My job was to bring in wood that my brother split and to throw it into a big pile. At first it was fun. Later I did gardening and helped my mother with canning. I went to school in a buggy or on horseback, and in a caboose in winter. I remember Father hitching the horse to our caboose, and Mother heating up some stones to keep our feet from freezing. One day, coming home in a snowstorm, we became lost, but our horse, Prince, knew the way and saved our lives.

As a child, I went to a Baptist church about ten miles away. I enjoyed the choir and learned to play the piano, although I was not encouraged to excel in music, because there were so many chores to do. At school, a kind teacher recognized my artistic abilities, and I began doing sketches and portraits. I entered a portrait in a contest and was awarded a prize of five dollars—a fortune! I realized that my work had worth, although my parents did not think that I could make a living as an artist. At age sixteen, I took up sewing and dress designing. I worked for a fashionable French dressmaker, where I met many women from high society and was fortunate enough to deliver a gown to the premier's wife and meet her for tea.

My youth was filled with many difficult and sad challenges. Two sisters of mine were born after I was twenty years of age. I made doll clothes and sewed nice clothes for them. I lived with a friend at that time, and we cooked our meals. I was part of the church and attended a week of vacation Bible school, where I was given a little New Testament. I not only read my Bible, but I wrote out many verses and taught them to girls in my girls' club. As a result of my teaching, the girls learned the Gospel and made their own little personal books with sketches in them.

Marriage and motherhood. I met my husband-to-be at a Bible camp. We were married and have five wonderful children, eight grandchildren, and nine great-grandchildren. Life has not always been easy for us, but we have been blessed and are happy in our faith and friendships in the church and community. I have continued with my seamstress work and my artwork and have shared it with many friends and family throughout the years.

Our family may not be perfect, but God is not finished with us yet.

The Golden Box

Paul Powers

"The Golden Box" has been excerpted from Paul Powers's autobiography, *Too Tough to Cry*. Many of you know that Paul is my husband—a successful children's evangelist, loving father, and beloved grandfather (Papa). But in December 1972, in the hallway of our Don Mills home, Paul's walk of faith hit a giant stumbling block. "The Golden Box" recalls that time in our lives. We hope it provides a "forgiving guidepost"—a reminder for us to carry on one step at a time. Paul's story begins with my introduction to his book.

INTRODUCTION
Margaret Fishback Powers

I HAD JUST BEEN speaking to a group of people (through an interpreter) in Tokyo, Japan, when one of the teachers at the college asked if I would explain more about my husband, Paul. In particular, he wanted to know why I had been fearful of marrying him, if he was such a wonderful Christian, as I had just said.

I talked a little bit about Paul's background—about his life before I met him. The gentleman said Paul's story was a true Christian testimony of real life. I have heard similar comments many times over the past years.

What was the deciding moment back there on the beach in Kingston, Ontario, so many years ago, that challenged me to claim this man as my husband?

It's like an instant freeze-frame movie in my mind, those moments on the beach where Paul and I walked and talked. He discussed his past and how God had carried him through so many troubles in his life, how he felt the strong presence of the Lord since coming back to his faith in the Savior.

Paul talked openly about his youth, about his fear of marriage and his disappointing previous relationships. How well I remember him saying, "Should you decide to marry me, I promise never to leave you. I promise with God's help to always be with you and never hurt you. I'll always treat you well."

I replied, "Paul, only Christ can make that promise to never leave us. He and He alone will be with us. His promises are kept; we can only try to keep ours."

That walk together in 1964 was for us the beginning of many, many long walks on beaches around the world and the start of the most fantastic journey of a lifetime. How could two people with such different backgrounds be cast together for a future of ministry?

One answer I have discovered through Paul is the power of true repentance and forgiveness; another is the strength of obedient determination. Over the years of our marriage, I have seen the struggles, failures, grief, and disappointments suffered by Paul, some caused by others. But I have also seen Paul's willingness to reach out in trust, in victory, in forgiveness, and with a renewed confidence in others. Words sometimes are repeated so often that their meaning can become limited or questionable. But Paul's challenges in everyday life have taught him to trust and to encourage, to get up to go on again and again—to reach up and call for help, yet to keep his accountability short with His Heavenly Father. If I were to limit my description of this man to a few words, I would say . . . he is a man after God's own heart, as King David of old. He learned to accept the unexpected and to forgive those who would put down the ministry he feels so deeply about—to forgive as he has been forgiven!

In Paul's story, you will find the thread of the poem "Footprints in the Sand," which I wrote in the dark hours of a new day when Paul asked me to marry him. You will see the maturing of faith and trust, the dark valleys of despair, the light of forgiveness, the assurance of the presence of God, and, though unseen, His guidance to those who would come to Christ Jesus on His terms, and His blessing to those who faithfully follow in "His footprints."

☙

THE GOLDEN BOX

SHIVERING IN THE DECEMBER COLD but burning with anger inside, I wearily trudged up the walk of my Toronto home. I had spent the most humiliating day of my life—begging churches for money they owed me.

Finances were tight that holiday season in 1972. My wife, Margie, and two daughters, Christina, four, and Paula, not quite two, were facing a bleak Christmas. Throughout the fall I had done children's crusades in at least eight churches in the Toronto area, but none had paid me at the time I spoke.

"We'll send you the offering in the mail," was the usual explanation. "We have to put it through our books first."

We had waited and waited, but no checks had come. Margie was pushing me for more money so she could get some of the household bills off her mind. We had business creditors who needed to be paid, and we also owed Margie's parents a sizeable amount of money they had given us as a loan earlier that year.

As Christmas approached, I got more and more frustrated and angry. I began to mutter about Christians who didn't pay their bills, when Margie said, "Well, stop complaining. Why don't you just go to the churches and tell them the truth? We need the money!"

It was December 23, and after breakfast I drove to the churches that were closest to our home, talking to pastors and church secretaries, but I was always told, "The check should be in the mail. Perhaps it's held up in the mail." Or, "I'm not sure about your check—I think it's waiting to be approved by the church treasurer."

"Look," I told the secretary at one church. "I'm practically broke. All I'm asking for is what the church owes me so my wife and two little girls can have a decent Christmas."

She opened the cash box in her desk drawer and took out a few dollars, saying, "I'm sorry, Mr. Powers, it's all I can give you without authorization from the pastor, but he won't be back until tomorrow night."

I replayed this same humiliating scenario all day long, getting a few dollars here and there, but no full payment from anyone. Instead, I often got looks that seemed to say, *You're in God's business—don't you trust God to provide?*

As I drove home I thought, *Yes, God does provide—He provides through His people, but if His people don't pay their debts, what then?* Along with the humiliation and anger, I felt spiritually dry and brittle. At Margie's insistence, I had been doing more speaking in churches instead of the magic acts in secular settings that always paid well. And now, what did I have to show for it? We had very little food in the house. In fact, lately Margie and I had been joining the girls in eating pablum because it was all we could afford.

At least tonight we'll have a decent meal, I told myself. *And when we get to the folks' farm on Christmas Eve, we'll eat like kings.*

Margie heard me come in and asked eagerly, "How did you do?"

"Not very well," I told her. "I went to eight different churches and collected less than forty dollars. I got gas for the trip to the farm. Here's some money for groceries and whatever else you need to pick up. Spend it carefully, Margie; it's all we've got."

Margie hid her disappointment and tried to maintain her usual cheery attitude as she bundled up the girls and they left to go shopping. She was glad to get out of there. I had been gone far longer than she had planned, and now I had come home frustrated and fuming—ready to blow up. As she left, I was looking around the living room to see what we might take to the pawn shop.

About two hours later, Margie and the kids returned, chattering excitedly about what they had bought. Margie was feeling good about some bargains she'd found at Christmas sales, but all I said was, "You're kidding! We can't afford to buy much more than a few groceries."

Margie stiffened and said coolly, "I spent the money on what I thought we needed."

I continued grumbling as we put things away, and then Tina showed me a roll of gold wrapping paper. "Look what Mommy got, Daddy."

I took the roll of paper, looked at it, and said, "What kind of special bargain is this?"

"Mommy got it for a dollar," said Tina proudly.

"A dollar! Well, I hope it's enough paper to wrap all the presents," was all I could think of. It turned out to be far less than that—just one sheet on a cardboard roll. And it had cost one entire dollar!

All the anger and frustration of the day boiled up in me and erupted.

"How could you be so wasteful?" I screamed at Margie. "You've simply thrown away a whole dollar on nothing—nothing but stupid wrapping paper. How could you do such a thing, Margie? I've been rationing dimes and nickels for weeks, just to have some money for gas to drive to the farm for Christmas."

Margie didn't say anything. She just looked crushed. Tina tried to look away and act as if nothing had happened.

A cold, depressing cloud hung over the dinner table that evening. With the groceries she had purchased, Margie was able to fix a fine meal, but everyone sat in stoic silence, barely picking at the food. Heads and shoulders sagged under the weight of my frustration and angry words. At one point Tina lifted her tearful blue eyes, surveyed my face, and then looked down at her plate again.

After dinner, we went downstairs to the bottom floor of our duplex, where I had my office. We had to finish some last-minute gift wrapping and other final preparations before leaving the next day to spend Christmas with Margie's family. Tina was there with us, but because I didn't want her to see us wrapping the dolls we had gotten at a bargain sale earlier in the year, I sent her out, saying, "Tina, would you go upstairs and get that gold paper your mother wasted the money on?"

I'm sure Tina didn't catch the full meaning of what I said, but Margie did. Margie knew I was trying to cut her down to size for being so "wasteful." Tina dutifully scampered off to find the paper while Margie and I continued wrapping presents, all the while bickering and picking at each other. I hadn't cut her down to size at all; I'd only undermined my own credibility as a husband and father. She defended her womanliness and right to buy what she felt was needed, and, of course, I defended my manliness by letting her know she was a bad manager.

"Oh yes, Paul," she snapped back. "You've got all the answers, don't you? You know everything."

Because Tina hadn't come back, I called upstairs but heard no answer.

"What's taking that kid so long?" I muttered as I stormed up the stairs with Margie right behind me. We came upon Tina in an alcove just off the living room, sitting in the middle of the floor, surrounded by wads of gold paper and three pairs of scissors. Gobs of sticky clear plastic tape were all over her as well as the rug. She had used up the entire single sheet of gold paper trying to wrap something that looked like a shoe box.

Tina smiled cheerfully as she saw us enter the room, but her smile turned to a look of terror as she saw the anger flooding my face. She sat wide-eyed and gave a pathetic little screech as I raced across the room, grabbed her by one arm, and jerked her right up into the air, slapping her hard several times.

Tina screamed in pain and terror as Margie stood there, horrified shock on her face. My head was spinning and I was practically incoherent, but Tina's screams and sobs made me realize what I was doing, and I stopped. My entire body began to shake, and suddenly other sounds flooded my mind—shouts of rage, anger, and pain that were locked in my memories of childhood. My thoughts flashed back to the innumerable times *I* had been the terrified child in the hands of a raging, drunken father.

I let go of Tina and she fell to the floor in a heap, still crying and hurt. Then I turned to Margie and tried to put the blame on her.

"Well, she deserved to be punished," I snapped. "And you know you shouldn't have wasted money on that wrapping paper." I sent Tina to her room as Margie stood there, disbelieving. Here was the man she had married, the man who had said he loved Christ and children; the man who had thanked God for being given a children's ministry. Now he was acting like someone possessed by a demon, terrorizing his own child and leaving her with bruises and handprints on her cheek where he had struck her.

Guilt flooded in and seemed to drown me in waves of remorse. *See,* the old memories whispered, *you're just like your old man . . . just like your no-good, drunken father who beat you and your brothers and sisters. You're a failure. You've failed in everything you've tried, and*

now you're going to fail just like your dad did when your mom died.
Now you're beating your child, smashing her, throwing her around and
shouting, just the way he used to do with you.

Despite the guilt, I didn't apologize to anyone. Tina had been
wrong; she had to learn. And Margie had to know I was head
of the house. She had to learn her place and that I had the right
to discipline the children. But even as I justified my position to
Margie, my mind kept telling me: *You liar, hypocrite. You haven't*
been set free from anything. You're living a fool's lie. You're just as bad
as your father was, and you've been trying to fool everybody. The real
Paul Powers is a guy who beats his children, just as his father did.

For the rest of the evening, our home was colder than the brisk
December night outside. Tina stayed in her room, and Margie
wouldn't even talk to me. Later I went in to talk to Tina, who
was still wide awake and looking frightened and sad at the same
time. What I said didn't comfort her: "How could you do such a
stupid thing? Don't you know how hard I worked for this money?
You know I was gone almost all day, just for a few crummy bucks!
How dare you! Aren't you sorry for what you did with the wrapping paper?"

Tina looked up at me and said in a tiny, trembling voice, "Yes,
Daddy, I'm s-s-sorry."

I didn't even kiss her good night. My arrogant pride just
wouldn't let me. I spent the night on the couch down in my
office. Margie had stood at the door to Tina's room and heard my

"good night" tirade. She didn't want anything to do with me—and I couldn't blame her. I tossed and turned all night long, never really falling asleep, only hearing the voices saying, *You're just like your father . . . you're a coward who beats little children . . . just like your father . . . you're no good, no good, no good . . .*

The next morning was the 25th, and we tried to begin the day as we always do—by having devotions and thanking the Lord. But the words stuck in my mouth, and my hurried prayer bounced off the ceiling. Margie was barely talking to me, but I still wasn't ready to apologize. I loved Margie, but my pride stood between us.

We were due to leave around ten, and we decided to go ahead and give the girls their dolls, which we had wrapped the night before. That way they would have something to play with on the hundred-mile drive to the farm. The girls opened their gifts at the breakfast table with squeals of delight. They seemed to have forgotten the terrible scene of the night before, but Margie hadn't and neither had I.

Then it was time to go. As we got on our wraps I watched Margie bundle both girls into their pink winter coats, the white fur on the collars framing their little cherubic faces. Usually I would have been bursting with pride about how cute they looked, but I was still carrying a huge leaden lump of anger that made every move difficult. I turned and almost tripped over the box Tina had wrapped in the gold paper. Irritably, I kicked it into the living room, not wanting to be reminded of the trouble it had caused. But Tina darted in, picked up the box, and ran back to hand it to me. The beautiful gold wrapping paper was crumpled and creased and torn in one corner. Plastic tape was plastered all over it, but although it looked marred, she gently held out her gift to me with loving pride.

"Here, Daddy, it's for you," she whispered, her blue eyes thoughtful and full of apprehension.

I grabbed the box from her tiny hands and noticed that it seemed quite light for its size. *What can it be?* I wondered. I shook it gently but could hear nothing rattle inside.

The lights from our Christmas tree made the rumpled gold paper sparkle in a rainbow of colors. Slowly I tried to open the box, but the tape just wouldn't give. The harder I tried to get it undone, the more frustrated I became. Glimpses of yesterday's horrible scene flashed across my mind. I felt guilt, sorrow—and anger. I wanted to apologize, but still, Margie and Tina had both been wrong. Margie had humiliated me, and kids simply have to learn to obey.

Finally, I impatiently ripped the box open, but when I looked inside, the same terrible anger boiled up in my chest. My neck and face became a prickly red. Doing my best to keep my temper, I turned to Tina and said sharply, "Christina! Don't you know you should put something in a box before you wrap it up as a gift?"

Tina didn't cower. She just looked up at me with tears streaming down her face. Again the voices in my mind whispered, *You're just like your old man . . . you beat your kids . . . you make them cry.*

But with seemingly no fear, only love, Tina said, "But, Daddy, I *did* put something in it. I blew kisses into it! It's full of love just for you!"

I stood there feeling a gut-wrenching shock go through my entire body. Then goose bumps started crawling all over me. The gold wrapping paper that still clung to most of the box was glowing with a strange and wonderful light. Even though Tina's golden box was empty, it was full. She had given me the gift that I needed most. In return for my anger and the painful slaps and abuse, she had given me a child's unconditional love.

My pride and anger melted right there in the hallway. I dropped to my knees, hugged Tina, and begged her forgiveness. I hugged Paula and Margie and begged their forgiveness as well, weeping uncontrollably. "I'm so ashamed. You deserve better than this. Why don't you leave me here at home and go down to the farm to see Grandma and Grandpa? I don't deserve any of you. You were right and I was wrong. It's my pride, my stupid pride. I'm so ashamed."

Margie smiled through her tears and the girls hugged me and kissed me. "Daddy, don't cry, we love you . . . Daddy, don't cry."

Tina said, "I'm sorry, Daddy, I'm so sorry."

"No, Tina, *I'm* sorry . . . Daddy's sick . . . Daddy's sick."

"Are you going to the hospital, Daddy?"

"No, but I'm going to go to the 'Healer.'"

The girls didn't understand, but Margie did. I held all of their hands in mine as we prayed together. I asked God to kill the enemy—my anger. I begged to be cured. I never wanted to lose my temper again—ever. I pleaded for healing because, outside of Jesus, nothing was more important. My family was my only world, and I wanted the enemy to die.

Margie knelt down beside me and said, "I forgive you. I'm to blame, too, because I've been upset and I've been nagging. I helped cause all of this, but we love each other and I know God's going to help us."

I clutched the golden box to my chest and said, "I'm going to keep this always. This is the best Christmas present of all."

Margie held our little girls tight and corrected me gently, "No, Daddy, Baby Jesus is."

"You're right, oh, you're right, Margie," I said. Then I turned and smiled at Tina, adding, "But this is the best Christmas present *I've* ever had, and we're going to have a lot more of them."

And I prayed it would be so. Only God could do it. He had brought me so far, from a horror-filled Christmas of long ago, through a life of crime, to Himself. He had given me the most wonderful family a man could want. My heart overflowed with thanks for the love of my children, for my wife, and for wisdom far greater than mine that, once again through a child, showed me what Christmas and love are all about.

Finding My Way

Margaret Fishback Powers

Among my saved newspaper clippings of articles I've found interesting or relevant is an item about a couple from the Nazarene church in Penticton, British Columbia. On their way to a combined holiday and conference in Nevada, they became tragically lost. It reminded me vividly of times when our maps were sketchy and we lost our way—everywhere from Australia to islands in the Caribbean—including one memorable trip during a hurricane. In my daily journeys I have sometimes stopped to seek direction from other Bible teachers. This reflection appeared in *Footprints: Scripture with Reflections for Women* (2004).

I always prided myself on being able to find my way around any city or town throughout the world. Paul would just give me a map and I would head out, perhaps with one of my children as co-pilot in the passenger seat, and be certain of finding my destination with ease. I found that this sense of direction gave me great freedom and independence.

When we moved to British Columbia, I seemed to have great difficulty in finding my way anywhere, and I had to put my faith in Paul and the map to take us across rivers and over winding mountain roads. Often, it all conflicted with my sense of where north, south, east, and west lay. I could not understand it; navigating had previously been so easy. Sometimes life can be much the same way; one minute you think you are on the right path and suddenly the path is filled with obstacles. When you become confused, remember you can ask God for directions.

Afterword

LOOKING BACK, GLANCING AHEAD

IN WRAPPING UP THIS TREASURY, I would like to quote four lines from the great nineteenth-century poet Henry Wadsworth Longfellow, one of my favorite writers. They remind us of life's accountability. These lines, which I learned as a child, are from the poem "A Psalm of Life":

> *Lives of great men all remind us*
> *We can make our lives sublime,*
> *And, departing, leave behind us*
> *Footprints on the sands of time.*

What many of us forget, however, is that great men—and women—have had to work very hard to accomplish their greatness.

Unfortunately, today it is acceptable to do as little as possible to get as much as possible. Some find a shortcut—let someone else do it for them—but get the recognition. That was not Longfellow's view of life. He held that work in itself was rewarding and led to a feeling of complete enjoyment.

I well remember the point my father used to make: if something is worth doing, it is worth doing right the first time. I have held this belief throughout my life, along with the feeling that quality of character is to be admired.

As I reflect over the years of ministry behind us and look forward to the work that remains to be done, I think of the words of my friend Dr. David Brown of Montego Bay, Jamaica:

"The person who would leave footprints on the sands of time will first have to wear work shoes!"

—Margaret Fishback Powers

Acknowledgments

I am extremely thankful to the many contributors for their skill and insights. In particular, I am indebted to the friends of *Footprints* from around the world whose input enhanced the project along the writing journey. I am most grateful to Brad Wilson and Dan Liebman for their ongoing encouragement and invaluable assistance over this past year. Finally, I wish to thank all my friends at HarperCollins, my publisher. Over the years, they have shared the gifts of kindness and friendship— the very threads that weave their way throughout this book.

We would love to hear from you!

We hope you enjoyed these stories that were inspired by or reflect the themes of "Footprints in the Sand." If you would like to submit a story for a future *Footprints* book, please contact:

Margaret Fishback Powers
c/o HarperCollins Canada Ltd.
2 Bloor Street East, 20th floor
Toronto, Ontario
M4W 1A8

Contributors

PART ONE: COMPASSION

A Poem for Arthur © 2015 by Arthur Thompson. Used by permission of Arthur Thompson.

Roses Are Red © 2015 by Eva Schatz. Used by permission of Eva Schatz.

The Pharmacy © 2015 by Alan Baker. Used by permission of Alan Baker.

The Letter Writer © 2015 by Charles Mueller. Used by permission of Charles Mueller.

Life Lessons © 2015 by Hilda Weill. Used by permission of Hilda Weill.

A True Florence Nightingale © 2015 by Lois Simpson. Used by permission of Lois Simpson.

Finding a Doctor © 2015 by Jane Serlin. Used by permission of Jane Serlin.

The Caregiver © 2015 by Vincent Rosner. Used by permission of Vincent Rosner.

PART TWO: HOPE, TRUST, AND FAITH

Carried through Grief © 2015 by Roberta A. Neault. Used by permission of Roberta A. Neault.

A Second Chance © 2015 by Jody Bergsma. Used by permission of Jody Bergsma.

A Pair of Sandals © 2015 by Dan Liebman. Used by permission of Dan Liebman.

Sometimes I Walk on Water © 2015 by Michelle Holmes. Used by permission of Michelle Holmes.

I'm Not Alone © 2015 by George Schmidt. Used by permission of George Schmidt.

The Three Bells © 2015 by Steve Connolly. Used by permission of Steve Connolly.

Do Not Fear, I Am with You © 2015 by Joy Gove. Used by permission of Joy Gove.

Through Happiness and Sorrows © 2015 by Joyce Bilton. Used by permission of Joyce Bilton.

Carried as on the Wings of an Eagle © 2015 by Lesley Anthea Lewis. Used by permission of Lesley Anthea Lewis.

PART THREE: BURDENS, COURAGE, AND STRENGTH

Another Day © 2015 by Faye Dewhurst. Used by permission of Faye Dewhurst.

The Shrouded Moon © 2015 by Marilyn Stremler. Used by permission of Marilyn Stremler.

Talking to the Children © 2015 by Sylvia Bosworth. Used by permission of Sylvia Bosworth.

Contributors

PART FIVE: KINDNESS AND COMFORT

The Real Spirit of Christmas © 2015 by Lois Simpson. Used by permission of Lois Simpson.

The Kindness of Strangers © 2015 by David Ross. Used by permission of David Ross.

A Perfect Cup of Coffee © 2015 by Tina Sullivan. Used by permission of Tina Sullivan.

This Little Light © 2015 by Cory Leon. Used by permission of Cory Leon.

Look After Your Kids © 2015 by Andrea Palmer. Used by permission of Andrea Palmer.

On a Hot Day in August © 2015 by Emma Bell. Used by permission of Emma Bell.

It Only Takes a Moment © 2015 by Janet Stein. Used by permission of Janet Stein.

Comfort Foods © 2015 by Bonnie Thompson. Used by permission of Bonnie Thompson.

Elijah's Cup © 2015 by Ellyn Jacoby. Used by permission of Ellyn Jacoby.

Guardian Angels Come in Many Disguises © 2015 by Ann Woollcombe. Used by permission of Ann Woollcombe.

PART SIX: FRIENDSHIP

A Letter to a Friend © 2015 by Arden and Jean Robertson. Used by permission of Arden and Jean Robertson.